Destination Champagne

The independent traveller's guide to Champagne
the region and its wines

A trip to Champagne would be nice,
Go once and you'll want to go twice;
The Countryside's fine,
The wine is divine,
And the people are awfully nice.

Philippe Boucheron

Published in 2005 by Wine Destination Publications Limited,
Designed by Blackberry and printed in England by Arron Print Limited, of Redditch.
Baskerville2 9/12pt
© Philippe Boucheron & Nick Mendes MMIV
ISBN 0-9549799-0-7

Front Cover: © John Hodder / Collection C.I.V.C

Acknowledgments

Guidebooks do not write themselves, nor do their authors sit down at their computers and the words appear as if by magic. This book is the sum of much research over many years, and the help and assistance of many colleagues whose friendship I value.

My grateful thanks are due to Françoise Peretti of the London office of the Champagne Bureau who was enthusiastic and supportive from the moment I first mentioned the idea to her. Philippe Wibrotte and Valérie Dubois from the Epernay office of the CIVC, Laurence Prevot of the Champagne Ardenne Comité Régional du Tourisme in Châlons-en-Champagne who made so many arrangements in France for me, and Stéphanie Chent-Tissier of the Aube-en Champagne tourist board in Troyes for all her help in the Aube. To Air France, EuroTunnel plc, and P&O Ferries for helping me over and under the Channel when I needed to be at the other side. To Tom Stevenson, the most knowledgeable of all champagne writers, for his generous advice and help and for allowing me to make free with all the valuable information in his seminal Encyclopaedia of Sparking Wine published by Christie's. To the International Wine & Food Foundation of America for permission to reproduce excerpts from my book on Growers' Champagne that it published in 2000. To my very good friend, gourmet, fellow wine writer and champagne enthusiast Michael Edwards for kindness and support. And last, but by no means least, to another very good friend and colleague, Neil Fairlamb for painstakingly reading my drafts and providing so many wise suggestions on how they could be improved by both additions and subtractions. To all of you, a heartfelt 'thank you'. This is as much your book as it is mine

Philippe Boucheron
Droitwich Spa, February 2005

Whenever you're drinking champagne,
Remember it's more than a name.
It isn't by chance
It all comes from France,
And quality's key to its fame.

This book is dedicated to all those hundreds of wine tourists that I have been fortunate enough to take out to Champagne over the years for Arblaster & Clarke, Grape Expectations and others, with grateful thanks for all that they taught me.

Contents

© *Valerie Dubois/Collection C.I.V.C*

Introduction

*Whenever I'm tired or in pain
I seek solace from Dr. Champagne.
The balm of his bubbles
Soothes away all my troubles
And soon I am back, right as rain.*

C hampagne, the world's most glamourous sparkling wine, is a magnet that attracts visitors from all over the world. *Destination Champagne* is a practical guide for the independent traveller visiting, or just passing through, the Champagne region of France. The name is derived from the Latin *campus*, meaning a plain, but there are in fact two champagnes; *La Champagne* is the countryside while *le champagne* is the wine. The guide will help the casual visitor learn about *La Champagne*, as well as enabling the wine enthusiasts to discover more about *le champagne*.

Most of the region lies within the province of Champagne Ardenne. However, there is a small part, closest to Paris and around Château-Thierry, which is in the Department of the Aisne. It is a diverse area, as rich in history as it is in wine, whose fertile rolling countryside combines vines and grain, grazing cattle and woods and whose visitor-friendly towns offer tourists of all ages the warmest of welcomes and the fondest of memories.

Tasting in the cellars
© *CDT Champagne Ardenne*

Champagne has become a prime destination for short holidays, attracting visitors from all over Belgium, France, Germany, Great Britain and the Netherlands. In addition, British holidaymakers passing through on their way by road to the Alps for winter sports, or in summer to the Mediterranean for sea and sun, often stop to visit a champagne producer and pick up a few bottles on their way.

Le champagne comes from the Marne valley, the Mountain of Reims and the Côte de Blancs, as well as the not so well-known Côte des Bar in the Aube which is nearer Chablis than it is

© Huyghens Danrigal/C.I.V.C Collection

Epernay. The natural centres for visitors are Epernay and Reims in the north and the historic half-timbered city of Troyes in the south. But it is worth following the well-signposted wine routes to discover tiny towns and villages nestling in the folds of the hills. Here you will find small growers producing their own champagnes as well as picturesque churches and a whole host of unusual things to do and places to see.

The guide has separate sections for each of the four principal wine-producing regions and their main towns. It provides sketches of champagne houses, winegrowers and co-operatives who welcome visitors and speak some English, as well as a small selection of hotels, B&B or *chambres d'hôte* and restaurants, together with places of interest worth visiting.

© Drappier Collection

A € symbol indicates a visit to a champagne house for which an admission charge is made; these may well vary with the number of wines being tasted and there will be discounts for children. Almost all the museums and other attractions charge for admission.

Getting to Champagne

Paris
Area of Champagne

FRANCE

Champagne, a most bountiful blessing,
Should always be crisp and refreshing.
With your glass not quite filled
And served moderately chilled,
It's better than beer, and no messing!

Many British visitors go by car, either taking the 35-minute trip under the Channel on the Shuttle, cruising across on a ferry or hovercraft to Calais or the SpeedFerries service to Boulogne.

People living beyond London and the south east of England can fly from their local airport to Paris and pick up a hire car for a champagne-packed weekend. They can often be in Epernay or Reims within three hours of take-off; many airlines offer attractive off-peak fly-drive packages that may even include accommodation. Londoners can also catch the train from Waterloo direct to Paris, Gare du Nord, where they can pick up a hire car at the station.

© Dover Harbour Board

The Route from the Channel

Travellers crossing over or under the Channel are on the autoroute almost as soon they leave the docks or rail terminal. You simply follow signs for Reims 270km (168 miles) away-allow three hours, which includes time for a 20-minute break.

Just beyond Calais, where the main feature is a giant sugar-beet factory, you are crossing historic ground. This is where, in 1520, Henry VIII of England met Francis I of France at the Field of the Cloth of Gold to try to resolve their wars.

Your journey takes you along the Western Front of the 1914-18 war, past towns that saw some of the

© Eurotunnel

bloodiest fighting. St-Omer is where the British armies had their HQ while Béthune was once at the centre of France's thriving coal mining industry – look out for the ski slopes on the old slag-heaps. Just before Arras, on your left, are what are left of the 60,000 Canadian Fir trees, one for each Canadian soldier killed in 1917 fighting for possession of Vimy Ridge; a most poignant war memorial where the shell-marked ground and trenches have been left for nature to reclaim.

Arras is a great place for an overnight stop, especially on a Tuesday or Friday night, as you will then be able to visit the market held every Wednesday and Saturday morning. The old Flemish-style town has a number of hotels including the comfortable Univers, with its secure car parking and good restaurant, and the simple but adequate 3 Luppas that is right on one of the two market squares.

Leaving Arras your route takes you past signs to Cambrai and St-Quentin. If you are driving though then take a break at the Les Arcs service station at Urvillers, just beyond the South St-Quentin junction. It is around 180km from Calais and should take you around two hours.

On your right, some 36km past the service station, you'll see a town with a large church,

Canadian War Memorial
© Veteran Affairs Canada

high on a hill. This is Laon that was, from the 8th to the 10th centuries, the capital of France. It had been a Roman city and it still has a number of medieval and renaissance buildings. The cathedral rises a majestic 52m from entry to top of its towers; seven were planned but only four were built. A cable car gives easy access to the old town. It runs up from beside the railway station where you can park your car.

The Route from Paris

Paris's Charles de Gaulle airport is well placed for getting to Champagne. You leave by the A1/E19 towards Paris, forking left on to the A3/E15, then follow signs for Marne la Vallée and the A4/E50.

Visitors arriving in Paris by Eurostar can pick up their hire car at the Gare du Nord. Leaving the station you should head east towards the Place de la République and then follow signs to Charenton where the A4/E50 begins.

You are now well on your way, less than 150km (93 miles) to Epernay or Reims. You will be travelling along the valley of the Marne that joins the Seine at Charenton. This is the route taken in 1914 by those Paris buses and taxis when they ferried soldiers to the front, 116km away at Dormans, after the German army broke through and their guns could be heard in the city. Your drive will take you past the town of Meaux, famous for its Brie which, while not actually made in *La Champagne*, is very much part of its gastronomy.

The next town of note is Château-Thierry, where the champagne trail begins. Travellers for Epernay leave us at junction 20 and, bypassing the town, follow signs for Epernay and the N3. Their route follows the river with vineyards on either bank, through Dormans on the way to Epernay – the capital of *le champagne*.

For Reims you keep on the autoroute running alongside the Canal du Marne which bisects the city.

Driving in France

Advice from the RAC

1. Remember to drive on the right and wear your seat belt at all times.

2. Get your car serviced a week before you depart: most breakdowns occur on the journey out or back when fully laden vehicles are travelling at sustained high speeds.

3. By law you must carry a warning triangle and a spare set of bulbs. Get them when your car is being serviced.

4. Fuel cans; full spare fuel cans are not permitted on the Shuttle or Ferries.

5. Vehicles powered by LPG are not allowed on the Shuttle.

6. Speed limits:

Toll motorways		dry	130kph/80mph
		wet	110kph/68mph
Cars	Other dual carriageways	dry	110kph/68mph
		wet	80kph/50mph
Urban driving			50kph/31mph
Fog – visibility less than 50m			50kph/31mph

7. Always give way to traffic coming from the right.

8. Fines: The police are empowered to collect on-the-spot fines of up to 350 euros and, if you haven't got it on you, they will escort you to a cash machine to get it!

9. If you have a new-style European number plate you won't need a GB sign: if you haven't then remember to place it on the left rear of your car – the outside corner.

10. Finally, don't drink and drive; the French limits are more severe than those in the UK and are even more strictly enforced.

© Air France

Additional Fly-drive Advice

1. Don't forget your driving licence: you won't get your car without it! The photo-card is accepted in France and also provides a means of identification.

2. Take time to get acquainted with your car before you leave the car hire company's site.

3. Check the car over for damage before you drive away.

4. Understand the insurance cover that the hire agreement includes and check the excess charges.

5. Before you depart find out the company's fuel policy for returning cars: it costs less to return it with a full tank.

Autoroutes

France operates toll autoroutes. Payment is either by coins, cash or credit card; or you push a button and receive a ticket that you hand in at the end of the section and then pay by cash or credit card; you do not sign the credit card receipt. Sections around main towns are free.

There are plenty of stopping places; these are '*aires*' or just somewhere to pull off the road, under the trees, to relax and there will be a rudimentary toilet. There are also petrol stations with small shops and decent toilets; the prices of their fuel and distance are shown on signs along the autoroute. Finally there are service stations with petrol, excellent toilets, good food and a calm restful environment – Les Arcs is quite the best on the champagne trail.

Sleeping & Eating in Champagne

Before you sit down at the table
To eat as much as you're able,
To get into the mood,
Before all that food,
Have a bottle of Lanson Black Label.

Chambre d'Hote
© Champagne Tarlant

Hostellerie La Briqueterie
© Hostellerie La Briqueterie

There is no shortage of fine places to eat and sleep in La Champagne. Indeed, visitors are spoilt for choice. There are, of course, elegant luxury hotels – some with Michelin-starred restaurants – as well as a wide selection of two and three star hotels, a number of which have excellent restaurants. Well-placed signs in cities and towns direct travellers to the hotels of their choice.

But why not discover the real Champagne by staying at one of the numerous chambres d'hote (bed & breakfasts), many run by champagne winegrowers and their families. These are often as well or better equipped and more spacious than two-star hotels and their breakfasts are invariably a delight.

A number of *chambres d'hote* also offer dinner which must be booked in advance. These meals, which invariably include wine, range from a simple but sustaining repast to a gourmet experience. Some wine farmers may offer you a glass or two of their *rebêche* with your meal. This is a still wine, made from what was left over from the press, which is normally sent to the distillery. It is not for sale but given to the workers, or members of a co-operative, for drinking at home.

If you are going out to dinner then the chances are that before you leave your host will invite you to share a bottle of their own champagne as your apéritif. And if you enjoy it, then they will be more than happy to sell you a few bottles to take home.

Restaurant Cellier aux Moines
© Ph Praliaud/CDT Aube

Small towns and villages may also have a country inn. More often than not it will be a small restaurant with a few simple, inexpensive and sometimes basic bedrooms.

Eating out in restaurants is one of the real pleasures in France. Most of them are small establishments that buy local produce and are proud of the part they are playing in maintaining France's reputation for fine food and wines.

But do remember that the French live to eat – while the British are said to eat to live – so be prepared to spend a great deal longer over a meal than you do at home. This is because the food will be cooked specially for you and not taken from a fridge and micro-waved. Many people eating in French restaurants remark on the absence of both soups and green vegetables. Both of these are eaten regularly in the home so they are not that often found on restaurant menus.

© Hotel Royal Champagne, Champillon

You can eat quite economically from the selection of two or three table d'hôte (fixed priced menus) that most restaurants offer. These must be displayed on the outside of the premises so that you can read them through before choosing where to eat. It may be necessary to reserve a table in popular restaurants and your hotel or *chambre d'hôte* host will be pleased to do this for you. They will even advise you on where to eat and what to choose when you get there.

The easiest way to reserve accommodation, a restaurant or a visit to a wine cellar is simply to telephone. Speak slowly, don't shout and be prepared to spell your name phonetically, preferably using French town names for each letter – 'A' for Amiens, 'B' for Bordeaux, 'C' for Calais etc. Hotels and many

Royal Champagne at night
© Royal Champagne

chambres d'hôtes are on E-mail and if you have access to a computer this might be easier. The guide shows all telephone numbers as if you are phoning from France. From outside France omit the zero

© CDT Aube

and prefix with 00 33, so the telephone numbers in the Marne become 00 33 3 26 etc.

Service charge at restaurants is invariably included in the price – look for the words *Touts Compris* or the initials *TTC* – so there is no need to tip but a few coins are always gratefully received as a sign that you have enjoyed the meal and appreciated the service.

An all-embracing guide of this nature cannot hope to provide a complete selection of hotels, inns or *chambres d'hôte*. However, the regional tourist offices, details of which are included at the end of the book, produce up-to-date brochures each year – many of these are printed in English – and they will be pleased to send them to you.

I drink Champagne when I am happy,
and when I am sad.
Sometimes I drink it when I'm alone.
When I have company I consider it obligatory.
I trifle with it if I am not hungry,
and drink it when I am.
Otherwise I never touch it ... unless I am thirsty.

Madame Lilly Bollinger

The Story of Le Champagne

Champagne's most glamourous start
Was due in whole, or in part,
To a draper in Reims,
And his uncle, it seems;
Their names were, of course, Ruinart.

© *Drappier Collection*

There are just 34,000 hectares (ha) to the east of Paris, of which about 31,000ha are planted, and these provide all the world's champagne – an average of 280 million bottles with an absolute maximum of 310 million bottles a year. The area is reduced because of the space occupied by buildings and roads as well as vineyards being replanted and not yet in production.

Originally the wine was made either by farmers from grapes harvested from their own vineyards or by monks in the many abbeys and monasteries that once thrived across France. The revolution of 1789 dissolved these religious houses and their lands were passed on to landowners to farm. Over the years the champagne industry has evolved from an ecclesiastical poly-culture into a highly sophisticated viticulture.

Krug in the 1920's
© *Krug*

The ownership of the land is just one part of a most elaborate system that includes how the grapes are grown and the wine made, all of which is controlled by the most rigorous and strictly-enforced rules and laws designed to ensure quality over quantity. Some 15,000 growers, around 2,200 of whom also make their own champagnes, own most of the vineyards. Few of these farmers have more than 5ha with the vast majority possessing a hectare or less. In addition, between them the 256 merchant houses own 4,200ha which is only sufficient for around 13% of their total needs.

The majority of the growers sell their grapes to the merchant houses, often with the help of brokers

© *Drappier Collection*

called *courtiers en vins*, or are members of the 57 co-operative wineries. These either make and market their wines or return newly-bottled champagne to the growers for ageing and marketing themselves. Merchant houses account for some 70% of all champagne sales of which 20% is from the winegrowers and 10% from the co-operatives.

Control and supervision

Some giant 'super-co-operatives' market their own brands under names such as Veuve A. Devaux, Nicolas Feuillatte, Jacquart and Pannier. These brands are becoming as well known as those of the major merchant houses which makes it difficult to tell a wine's provenance. However, two small letters printed with some numbers at the bottom of the label establish the source of every bottle of champagne:

NM	stands for négociant-manipulant, a champagne house or merchant who buys in most, or all, of its grapes,
RM	is a récoltant-manipulant or winegrower who makes his champagne from grapes grown in his own vineyards,
CM	cooperative de manipulation, champagne entirely produced and marketed by co-operatives,
RC	récoltant-coopérateur, wines made by a co-operative and returned to the farmer to mature, disgorge and sell,
MA	is marque d'acheteur or Buyers own Brand,
SR	stands for société de récoltants, a family company of winegrowers.

The number after these letters identified the individual producer.

Quality control at Nicolas Feuillatte
© *Champagne Nicolas Feuillatte*

The industry is controlled and supervised by a combination of official government and representative bodies. The most important and powerful of these is *l'Institut National des Appellations* or INAO. This is the government organisation that has overall responsibility for controlling the strict appellation legislation from harvest to bottle. All champagne producers have to be able, at all times, to provide a complete audit trail that follows the grapes harvested (not more than 10,400kg per ha) to the juice produced (not more than 2,550 litres from every 4,000kg) to the bottle. And this even includes the wine lost during the dégorgement when the dead yeast sediment is ejected from the bottle. Even this is saved and sent to a distillery for turning into brandy.

INAO officials can come into a cellar at any time and select six bottles at random from a specific batch that is maturing on its sides. These will be sealed and labelled; one bottle will be taken away for laboratory analysis and the others left with the producer. If the test sample fails to come up to the minimum standard laid down then another bottle will be tested. If that also fails then the whole batch will be confiscated and destroyed with the producer having no recourse; they just lose the wine and the income that it would have generated.

Traditional Coquard Press
© CDT Champagne Ardenne

There are a number of regional organisations that interrelate at various levels in what might first appear to be a bureaucratic maze of Byzantine proportions. But in fact each represents a sector of the business with the *Comité Interprofessionnel du Vin de Champagne* – or CIVC-based in Epernay providing the umbrella body for the whole industry and a forum within which winegrowers, merchant houses and co-operatives can meet and share their common interests. Among other things the CIVC is responsible for research and setting the dates for the harvest.

Before the European Commission stopped the practice in 1990, the CIVC also fixed the price of the grapes at harvest. Today, before harvest, a benchmark figure is agreed for five years following consultation between representatives of the wine farmers and merchant houses.

The winegrowers' organisation, *le Syndicat Général des Vignerons*, is also based in Epernay. This looks after their specific interests in the vineyard, winery and market.

Krug's barrels
© Champagne Krug

In 1882 the big merchant houses established their own organisation, *le Syndicat des Grandes Marques*. *Grandes Marques* simply means big brands and should not be confused with Grand Cru or great growths, those villages rated at 100% in the *échelle des crus* (page 24). The *Syndicate* was finally dissolved in 1997, following its inability to agree which houses still maintained sufficient quality to remain *Grandes Marques*. Its place has been taken by *l'Union des Maisons de Champagne* (Union of Champagne Houses) which currently has some 24 members representing 60% of all the champagne sold by the 256 merchant houses.

Maintaining barrels at Bollinger
© Champagne Bollinger

© Frédéric Hadengue/Collection C.I.V.C

As champagne's popularity increased in the 19th century so an industry evolved with large merchant houses buying in their grapes from the farmers. Later, in the 1930s and more recently in the 1950s, co-operatives were founded, with financial assistance from the government, to encourage growers to combine together to make and market their wines.

However the essence of champagne, like all other French wines of quality, is to be found in its *terroir* – that magical mixture of soils, aspect to sun and mesoclimate – for which there is no satisfactory word in English. The story of champagne is a never-ending saga of men and women dedicated to perfection. Only their determined, single-minded pursuit of excellence enables a truly great wine to be created in such a northerly latitude. And they do it all from vines planted in a thin layer of soil over chalk.

This chalk provides perfect drainage while retaining sufficient moisture to allow the grapes to feed and develop, even in a dry summer, while in wet summers it absorbs all the excess moisture, keeping the vineyards more or less dry. The chalk also stores and reflects the heat of the sun. The roots of the vines drive deep into their hostile home seeking sustenance and those special minerals and trace elements which give champagne its delicacy and finesse.

The chalk in the north of the region – around Reims and Epernay – is made up from billions and billions of tiny fossilised sea creatures such as belemnites, mircrasters and urchins. These once lived in a vast sea that ran from the White Cliffs of Dover to hills beyond Epernay. Slowly the sea retreated and then, some 30 million years ago, there was the first of two massive earthquakes that between them lifted up and ruptured the seabed.

As the seasons eroded the land, soil filled the ground between the chalk outcrops. In time this became the fertile pastures on which cattle feed and crops are grown while the south-easterly facing chalk slopes provide the ideal home for vines.

Vines have been planted in *La Champagne* since the first century AD. For hundreds of years the kings of France were crowned in Reims cathedral and, as a result, the region's wines were much favoured at court. However, it was not until the 17th century that *le champagne* as we know it today was created.

Dom Pérignon and Dom Ruinart

For this bounty, legend tells us, we should be eternally grateful to two Benedictine monks, Dom Pierre Pérignon, who is often incorrectly credited with inventing the process, and Dom Thierry Ruinart who helped found the first champagne house. Their names live on today with Dom Pérignon being Moët & Chandon's *Cuvée de Prestige*, while Ruinart – also part of the Moët-Hennessy combine – creates elegant, stylish champagnes.

Dom Ruinart from an early portrait
© *Champagne Ruinart*

Towards the end of the 16th century wine makers in the region began to notice that, during the summer following the harvest, the wine would sometimes start a second fermentation in the bottle. It was the administrator of the Abbey of Hautvillers, on the hills overlooking Epernay, who perhaps first studied this phenomenon. His name was Dom Pierre Pérignon.

His lifelong application to le champagne led him to develop the art of the Cuvée: blending wines from different vineyards, grapes and vintages to create superbly balanced wines. He, and other monks, began to give their wines a second fermentation in their bottles to make them, as Dom Pérignon put it, 'sparkle like the stars in the sky'.

Taittinger cellars
© *Champagne Taittinger*

This was only made possible because at that time in the north of England glass bottles were being made from furnaces fired by coal rather than wood. This was to help conserve the forests for timber for building warships. These new bottles were strong enough to withstand the high pressure which, in a bottle of champagne, is around six atmospheres or three times that of a car tyre. Even then, small faults in the glass would create a weakness and bottles would suddenly explode when the pressure built up as they were lying on their sides. This still occasionally happens but at one time cellar workers had to wear gloves reinforced with steel and wire mesh masks, like fencers, to protect them from flying shards of glass.

At the same time Portuguese merchants were travelling across Europe selling their new cork stoppers. Held in by string, these could contain the immense pressure of the sparkling wine.

Dom Pérignon
© *Moët & Chandon*

Among Dom Pérignon's close friends was a fellow Benedictine monk from Reims, Dom Thierry Ruinart. We are told that Dom Pérignon gave Dom Ruinart some bottles of his sparkling wine. Now, or so the story goes, Dom Ruinart was not all that fond of wine; but his nephew was. His name was Nicolas Ruinart and he was a successful linen draper in Reims. Nicolas was so impressed with the wine that he found out from his uncle how it was produced and in 1729 started the very first champagne house.

Barrel storage at Nicolas Feuillatte
© Champagne Nicolas Feuillatte

Today champagne is still made in very much the same way as that developed by Dom Pérignon and his fellow monks. The main difference is perhaps the variety of grapes employed. We don't know for sure what Dom Pérignon used but since 1935 the wine may only be made from one white and two black grapes – Chardonnay, Pinot Meunier and Pinot Noir – all grown and harvested by hand within *La Champagne*.

Stainless steel tanks
© Champagne Lanson

It is remarkable that a wine so transparently golden is made, in great part, from black grapes. This is because all the colour pigment lies in the skin and not the flesh. Hand picking the grapes into small plastic boxes helps protect them from damage. They are then gently pressed, close to the vineyard, using traditional basket, bladder or pneumatic presses or the new inclined plate presses. Immediately after pressing the skins are removed to ensure that there is no hint of pink in the unfermented juice, or *must*.

The precise areas in which the vines may be planted, their distance apart and the methods of trellising are all strictly laid down and controlled. As indeed is the yield at harvest time and the amount of juice that may be extracted from the press. The freshly pressed juice is allowed to rest overnight, often chilled, for any solids to drop to the bottom of a tank before it is taken to the winery for its first fermentation.

Two fermentations

Champagne is a fine wine of great quality made in the most northerly latitude with a continental climate that can be hot in summer and cold in winter. Before global warming, cool summers meant that the grapes would not have fully ripened, so the wine is fermented twice.

Deposit in the bottle
© Collection C.I.V.C

The first fermentation of the base wine takes place at harvest time in large stainless steel vats or oak barrels. Sometimes, in the autumn, these wines are allowed to undergo a natural bacteriological transformation that changes harsh apple or malic, acids into softer lactic or milky ones. This is called the malolactic conversion – or malo – and can be started by inoculating with bacteria or simply allowing the temperature of the cellar to rise.

Each spring there are extensive and exhaustive tastings of all the vats which could be the produce of the three varieties of grape as well as numerous different vineyards, plots and pickings. These wines, including reserves from previous years, are selected and blended by mixing them in giant vats to create a desired house style for the top selling non-vintage styles. Vintage champagnes, however, are entirely made from the fruit of a single year.

These blends spend a short time to meld together with a mixture of cane sugar and yeast before the wine is then put into bottles. These are capped with crown corks and then stacked on their sides, 15 to 20 high and 40 to 50 or more deep, in huge cellars hewn out of the living chalk. Some of these cellars date back to Roman times when they were dug as quarries for the limestone used to build the city of Reims.

It is in these cool cellars, 30m below the ground where the temperature remains at around a constant 11°c, that the magical process that creates champagne takes place. First there is the *prise de mousse*, the second fermentation in the bottle, which is provoked by the yeast feeding off the sugar. This creates alcohol and carbonic gas which, because it can't escape, becomes trapped in the wine giving champagne its scintillating sparkle.

After an absolute minimum of 15 months for Brut – often longer and a number of years for vintage and *Cuvée Prestige* – the process is complete. But the wine is not yet clear; inside the bottle there is a deposit of sticky dead yeast cells which gives champagne its rich biscuity flavours. This has to be removed so that the wine can become clean and clear.

Remuage

This was once done by hand, employing a method developed in the early 19ᵗʰ century by one of champagne's long line of famous widows. She was Madame Clicquot-Ponsardin, better known as *la Veuve* (widow) *Clicquot*. Up to her time the bottles had been given a few perfunctory shakes and left to stand on their necks in sand for the deposit to drop. She had her kitchen table cut in half and then hinged together with holes cut into them at an angle. The bottles were then placed neck first into the holes. Today the *pupîtres* still used in the cellars are said to be based on her kitchen table.

Disgorging by hand
© Collection C.I.V.C.

Every few days experienced cellar-men, called *remuers*, will, with one deft movement, give each bottle a slight twist, a gentle shake, and move its neck a little further down. This is the *remuage* or riddling. Using both hands a skilled *remuer* can turn some 50,000 bottles a day. After six to eight weeks the bottles will be facing neck down with all the sediment resting on a plastic insert in the crown cork.

Modern technology is replacing this time consuming wrist-wriggling. Computer-controlled gyropallets, first developed in Spain and holding 500 bottles, do all the twisting and shaking required in a week.

Gyropallets
© Valérie Dubois / Collection C.I.V.C.

The neck of the bottle is now frozen in a brine solution, the crown cork removed and the gas pressure of up to six atmospheres (84psi) drives out the solid slug of iced sediment. This is the *dégorgement*. A quick sniff to ensure that the wine in the bottle is sound and it is topped up with the *liqueur d'expédition*, a solution of the same wine and cane sugar.

New corks are driven in, secured with a wire muzzle, a quick shake to mix the *liqueur* with the wine and the bottles are once again taken back to the cellar to rest on their sides for at least three months or more.

When the time comes for them to leave, the bottles are washed, labelled, dressed with their neck foil and shipped to customers all over the world.

Shaking after disgorgement
© Champagne Krug

Styles of Champagne

Wedding cakes are piled deck upon deck,
Brut Champagne their flavours will wreck.
For pure pleasure and joy,
And tastes that won't cloy,
You should always be served Demi-Sec.

Jean-Paul Gandon, Lanson's Chef de Cave, at work
© *Champagne Lanson*

C hampagne producers develop their own style that they strive to reproduce faithfully year after year. Although they all make a number of different qualities, by far the vast majority of bottles sold are non-vintage Brut. These dry champagnes are ideal for drinking any time, day or night. Many create *Blanc de Blancs*, which are made from white Chardonnay grapes, while others produce *Blanc de Noirs* from the black Pinot varieties.

From time to time some producers will create a champagne without adding sugar in the *dosage*; these are called by various names like *Brut Zero*, *Brut Sauvage* and *Ultra-Brut*. *Demi-Sec, Sec* or *Dry* and *Rich*, with their stronger sugar *dosage*, are sweet and ideal for toasting married couples with rich wedding cake or drinking with foie-gras.

Champagne *rosé* has traditionally been made by blending a little still red Pinot Noir, made in the region and known as a *Coteaux Champenois*, with the base wine before bottling for the second fermentation. However, a growing number of producers now create their rosé from a pink base-wine made by gently macerating Pinot grapes.

Vintage wines are those made from grapes of a single harvest and should represent the very best of a fine year. However, most champagne *cognoscenti* agree that the spirit of champagne is best expressed by non-vintage *cuvées* that contain reserve wines from previous years. The finest of these show the artistic mastery of the blender and his skill in assembling wines from so many vats, and reserve stock, to create a single harmonious wine.

Most producers, whatever their size, will have a *Prestige Cuvée* created from the pick of their best vineyards and finest vats. The most famous of these are created by the big houses and have such well-known names as Moët's Dom Pérignon, Lanson's Noble Cuvée, Roederer's Cristal, Veuve-Clicquot's La Grande Dame, Pommery's Louise and Taittinger's Comtes de Champagne. A number of winegrowers, ever eager to show what they can do, have created *Le Club Trésors* to show off their *Cuvées Prestige* (Page 27).

© *Champagne Pommery*

All champagne benefits from ageing on its dead yeast or lees. The longer a bottle rests maturing on this deposit before *dégorgement*, the fuller and richer will be the flavours. The young wines must be allowed to rest on their sides in the cellars long enough for their natural acidity to come into balance with the fruit. There are few things more unpleasant than 'green' champagnes, released before their time, that are still dominated by raw acidity.

Wines, like Alfred Gratien, Gosset and Lanson, which don't have a malolactic transformation, need longer for their initial acidity to come into balance with their fruit – and then they keep their freshness for a very long time. As a rule of thumb, however, champagne can be kept for as long as it rested on its first cork.

Canal at Mareuil sur Aÿ
© *Huyghens Danrigal/Collection C.I.V.C.*

Although sparkling champagne is the region's most important product, two still wines called coteaux champenois are produced, a white Chardonnay and a red from Pinot Noir, while in the Aube they produce *Rosé de Riceys*, a serious still fruity rosé that ages like Burgundy. In addition there is an interesting champagne apéritif made from unfermented grape juice blended with the local *eaux-de-vie* called *Ratafia de Champagne*. Finally there are two styles of *eaux-de-vie* produced by local distilleries. These are a fearsome *Marc de Champagne*, distilled from what was left in the press, and the more sophisticated *Fine de Champagne* that is made from the juice left over from the final pressing or the sediment from the disgorgement.

Champagne should always be stored on its side in a cool dark cellar and never disturbed until you are ready to open it. Any movement, even a gentle tapping of the cork, will excite the bubbles which tends to age the wine prematurely.

'A single glass of champagne imparts a feeling of exhilaration.
The nerves are braced; the imagination is stirred,
the wits become more nimble'.

Winston Churchill

The grape farmers' revolution

The second half of the 19th century was not kind to Champagne. In 1852 a terrible attack of oidium was followed in 1878 by mildew and then, in 1888, the dreaded phylloxera parasite arrived. This insect, which came to France from America via England, attacked the roots of the vines and decimated Europe's vineyards. In those days little was known about pesticides or the grafting of rootstock and the vineyards were all but destroyed.

The failure of the 1910 harvest, due to atrocious weather conditions, was followed by the merchant houses dropping the price for the grapes from 2.7 francs a kilo to one franc and even buying cheaper grapes from outside the region. This was more than the impoverished farmers could take and, in January 1911, thousands of them demonstrated in Damery and Epernay; the army was called out and almost opened fire. In April of the same year another rising in Aÿ saw the town barricaded, houses destroyed and 31 cavalry squadrons and 26 infantry companies were rushed in to quell the violence.

© *Museum Le Phare*

The Decree of 3rd June 1911 marked out the boundaries for the two controlled appellation zones of the Marne and the Aube. However it was not until 1930 and 1935 that the definitive rules were set down and agreed while the pruning system was not finalised until June 1938.

Champagne's Cru Classé System

After all day pleading in Court,
A lawyer will usually resort
To his glass of champagne,
While he tries to explain
The difference 'twixt crime and a tort.

Visitors to Champagne are surprised by how relatively little of the land is under vine. This is because the vines are planted on south-facing limestone or chalk slopes and the immediate neighbouring land. The deeper, more fertile soil is used for a combination of arable farming and raising cattle.

Winter pruning
© *John Hodder/Collection C.I.V.C.*

The vineyards in the north radiate from the Valley of the Marne. North and south of the river is the Montagne de Reims, where the vineyards loop around the hill between Reims and Epernay, while the Côte de Blancs runs for some 25km south of Epernay towards Sézanne.

The land to the south of Troyes, between the River Seine and its tributary the Aube, known as the Côte des Bar, is also limestone-based. But this is Kimmeridgian clay that can also be found 65km away in Chablis as well as Sancerre in the central Loire valley. This special clay, named after a village in Dorset, is rich in shale and can sometimes even be burnt as fuel.

The vineyards of Champagne are divided between 301 villages called *crus*, or growths. The *terroir* of these *crus* changes quite dramatically and those with the most suitable soils, aspect to the sun and climate will naturally produce the better grapes.

Grand Cru grower among his vines
© Champagne Marguet-Bonnerave

In 1911 the forerunner of the CIVC produced a list of 11 *crus* that it rated as 100%. In 1985 this was increased to 17 and these are the only villages that are allowed to call their champagnes *Grand Cru*. And then only if all the wine comes from *Grand Cru* villages.

A number of Grand Cru champagnes are produced by winegrowers fortunate enough to have vineyards in these areas. At the same time many of the *Grande Marque Cuvée Prestige* are also made almost exclusively from these top quality grapes. Many wine makers, particularly in the *Grand Cru* villages, prefer to create their champagnes from either pure Chardonnay – for *Blanc de Blancs* – or a blend of Chardonnay and Pinot Noir. This has tended to give Pinot Meunier a reputation as a 'lesser' grape.

Another 42 crus have been rated at between 99 to 90% and these are the *Premier Cru*. Grapes from the other 243 *Petit Cru* villages are rated between 89 and 80%. This is called *l'échelle des crus*, literally the ladder or scale of growths. Up until 1990 the true importance of the *échelle* lay in the fact that the price for the grapes was established before the harvest by the CIVC. Farmers in the *Grand Crus* received 100% of the agreed price while those in other villages were paid according to their position on the scale. Since then, although the price is set for five years to help stabilise the market, it is now left for the individual growers and houses to negotiate.

The Grand Cru Villages (>: indicates the original eleven)

Ambonnay >	Cramant >	Puisieulx
Avize >	Louvois >	Sillery >
Aÿ >	Mailly-Champagne >	Tours-sur-Marne >+
Beaumont-sur-Vesle	Mesnil-sur-Oger	Verzenay>
Bouzy >	Oger	Verzy
Chouilly > *	Oiry	

The Premier Cru Villages

99%	Mareuil-sur-Aÿ	Tauxiéres	
95%	Bergères-les-Vertus	Billy-le-Grand	Bisseuil
	Chouilly +	Cuis *	Dizy
	Grauves *	Trépail	Vaudmanges
	Vertus	Villeneuve-Renneville	
	Villers-Marmery	Voipreux	
94%	Chigny-les-Roses	Cormontreuil	Ludes
	Montbré	Rilly-la-Montagne	Taissy
	Trois-Puits		
93%	Avenay	Champillon	Cumières
	Hautvillers	Murtigny	
90%	Bezannes	Chamery	Coligny +
	Cuis *	Ecueil	Etrèchy +
	Grauves *	Jouy-les-Reims	Pargny-les-Reims
	Pierry	Sacy	Tours-sur-Marne *
	Ville-Dommange	Villers-Allerand	Villers-aux-Noeuds

+ = villages classified for black grapes only
* = villages classified for white grapes only

© *Champagne Lanson*

If you're willing to take my advice
Champagne at eleven is nice.
Whatever it is,
The fizz does its bizz',
But a night-cap? You'd better think twice.

The Champagne Vine-Growers Club

Dealers in Stocks and in Bonds
Are really most awfully fond
Of the glass of Champagne,
That just cures all that pain,
When they get it so terribly wrong.

For three centuries wine farmers in champagne have tended their vines and made fine sparkling wines. And, like farmers the world over, they enjoy showing off the best that they can produce.

The more important merchant houses could present their cuvée prestige as their flagships while growers could only stand and watch. However some 30 years ago a few got together to form *le Club de Viticulteurs Champenois* – the Champagne Vine-Growers Club, now known as *le Club Trésors de Champagne*, the Club of the Treasures of Champagne.

Harvesting
© *John Hodder/Collection C.I.V.C.*

© John Hodder/Collection C.I.V.C

This is a group of around 35 growers, all within the *Montagne de Reims, le Vallée de la Marne* and *Côtes des Blancs*, who have agreed voluntarily to be bound by a most rigorous charter that controls production. Each creates a *cuvée prestige* which, following approval by a tasting-panel of their members, is bottled into special traditional squat-shaped 'pot' bottles that are emblazoned with the club's badge of two winegrowers, set between a pair of *fleur-de-lys*, carrying a giant bunch of grapes, all set within the club's title.

You can invariably tell members of the club because they proudly display the badge on the outside of their premises and on all their literature. The one thing that you can be sure of is that their Special Club champagnes will indeed be very special. This is because the growers are bound to observe three essential principles; authenticity, rigour and originality. First the champagnes may only be made from grapes harvested from their own vineyards with the blend assembled under the ever-watchful eye of a qualified oenologist (wine scientist) from a most careful selection of the member's best *cuvées*.

What makes these wines so exceptionally special is that they are in every respect the fulfilment of every winegrower's ambition; the ultimate expression of their own *terroir*.

Visiting Champagne Producers

The nineties were naughty, they say,
Champagne Charlies were holding their sway.
They were awfully fond
Of La Belle Demi-Monde,
But drink from their slippers? No way!

T here can be few experiences more enjoyable than tasting champagnes in the cellars where they were created. This, after all, is the main reason why so many people keep going back, to visit old friends and make new ones!

Most, but not all, of the big merchant houses and co-operatives have organised visitor facilities that include well-trained uniformed staff and boutiques where you can buy their champagnes and other gifts. It is very much a public relations operation that enables consumers to get to know the house, understand its values and appreciate its wines. The charges for these visits vary depending upon the number and quality of the champagnes tasted at the end of the tour. At the smaller merchant houses and co-ops visits are given by members of the management team.

© *Champagne Tarlant*

Some leading producers such as Bollinger, Gosset, Charles Heidsieck, Krug, Lanson, Pol Roger, Roederer and Salon do not receive casual visitors. If you particularly wish to visit one of them, then the best way is to try and arrange it well in advance through your local wine merchant who stocks their champagnes.

Winegrowers are farmers who don't have large public relations budgets to support cellar tours. You will invariably be taken around by a member of the family who has plenty of other things to do but Champagne hospitality demands that while you are on their premises you are their honoured guest.

It is also important to recognise that they make their living from selling champagne and not taking visitors around. You will always be offered a tasting of one, two or more of their champagnes and,

© Benoit Marguet

if you like them, it is a wonderful opportunity to buy. You will find the winegrower's prices at the cellar door excellent value, costing less than the wines sold by the big merchant houses in their boutiques. However, if circumstances prohibit purchasing then it is only polite to explain this from the beginning and be prepared to pay a small charge for the visit and tasting. But do remember that, if you are travelling by air, champagne bottles are very heavy which is why they are invariably sold in cases of just six bottles.

The best advice is always telephone a winegrower first to make an appointment and do call back immediately if circumstances change and you can not keep the appointment. This is not only polite but also means that the family might be able to accommodate other interested visitors.

Growers' cellars are invariably cramped and the chalk from the walls can easily rub off on to clothing. Always wear flat shoes and remember that the constant 11°c temperature in the cellars makes them cool in summer and warm in winter, so dress appropriately.

As a courtesy to your fellow visitors, ladies should not wear strong toilet waters or scent and gentlemen should refrain from powerful after-shave lotions. This is because their perfumes will carry and interfere with the subtle aromas of the champagnes and the tasting pleasure of your companions.

As you drive around the champagne villages you will see plenty of signs inviting you to *déguster*, or taste. These producers are only too pleased to give you an opportunity of tasting their wines in the hope that you will be impressed and buy a few bottles. If your French is minimal then it is best only to stop at those who indicate that they speak English but don't be surprised if it is as basic as your French! More often than not they won't offer you a cellar tour because this takes up far too much of their time.

You should allow 1½ hours for a formal visit, more if you are buying, and up to 45 minutes to an hour for an informal tasting.

Finding your way around the villages is comparatively easy. This is because they all have directional signs with the names of all the winegrowers, producers, co-ops and *chambres d'hôte* while the principal villages are invariably located on one of the well-signed *Route des Vins*.

As you drive along the roads keep an eye out for the large Voie de la Liberté kilometre posts that look like large cream and red milestones. There are 12,000 of these symbolic markers, erected after the last war and stretching from the Normandy village of Sainté-Mère-Eglise to Metz and Bastogne. They trace the route taken in 1944 by U.S. General Patton's troops from the Utah landing beach towards Germany.

Lunch at an Auberge

Champagne is an excellent *apéritif*. It really does get the taste buds running and works up quite an appetite. One of the pleasures of visiting the growers in the morning is lunching afterwards in the local village auberge or inn.

The regional cuisine contains a great deal of river fish, in particular *brochet* and zander, pike and pike-perch. *Cervelas de brochet* are sausages made from pike and potatoes.

The pig contributes smoked hams and a great number of speciality sausages including *Andouillettes*, a rich and powerful tripe sausage made in Troyes, that takes a great deal of courage to eat!

Potée champenoise, a combination somewhere between a substantial soup and a hot-pot, is the traditional harvest-time dish served to the pickers at midday. It is made from pork with possibly a chicken or two, sausages, chunks of ham, autumn vegetables and potatoes.

Oysters have always been popular and go extraordinarily well with champagne.

La Champagne is also famous for her cheeses. Chaource, named after a town of the same name in the Aube, is a creamy soft cow's milk cheese that is light yellow and chalky when young but develops rich, nutty flavours when fully ripe. Langres is a wonderfully pungent creamy cow's milk cheese; a pretty yellow colour, it has the sweet aroma of lemons with a touch of bacon. Brie de Meaux, although not actually made in *La Champagne*, is not only a near neighbour but also one of France's Kings of Cheese. Soft and creamy, it should have a nutty flavour with hints of mushrooms.

In autumn *rousselet*, a rich and juicy pear that can't easily be packed, is delicious especially when accompanying Langres or a fully ripe Brie de Meaux.

Biscuits de Reims are small oblong macaroons and were once considered the correct accompaniment for champagne tastings, although if you are lucky you will be offered some Brioche. *Massepains de Reims* is another small oblong macaroon while *pain d'épice*, a spiced honey-cake, is another Reims speciality.

The Valley of the Marne

Winston Churchill did battle and toil,
The dark deeds of the Nazis to spoil.
While saving the nation,
His great relaxation
Was Pol Roger's expressive White Foil.

Since ancient times the valley of the River Marne has provided the main route between Paris, the Low Countries and north Germany. Invading armies and traders have all used this ancient highway. It has seen Roman legions and was Napoleon's route to the east; it was used by Bismarck in 1870 and by the Kaiser's armies in 1914.

The river Marne has always played a key role in Champagne. In the far-off days before roads and railways it was the highway along which wine and other regional produce reached Paris. Vines have been planted along the sides of the hills that follow the banks of this sinuous river since well before the Romans came.

VALLÉE DE LA MARNE

CHÂTEAU THIERRY

LA MARNE

DORMANS
OEUILLY
DAMERY
CUMIÈRES
HAUTVILLERS
CHAMPILLON
MUTIGNY
AVENAY
MAREUIL SUR AY
EPERNAY
BISSEUIL
TOURS SUR MARNE
CHÂLONS EN CHAMPAGNE

NOT TO SCALE

As the river winds along the valley so the chalk and soils change but, in the main, it is belemnite chalk covered with a mixture of clay and limestone with lignite and sandstone.

Although the river between La Ferté-sur-Jouarre and Châlons-en-Champagne is some 220km long, the more important vineyards lie in what is sometimes referred to as *la Grande-Vallée-de-la-Marne*. This runs the 36km between the village of Dormans, 25km west of Epernay, to Tours-sur-Marne.

Pinot Meunier is the principal grape grown along the Vallée-de-la-Marne, although both Pinot Noir and Chardonnay are also planted.

Many champagne producers are reticent about using Pinot Meunier, even though it is a valuable grape that matures early, adding rich red fruit flavours to the blend. Some of them are experimenting with *Blanc de Noirs* made entirely from Pinot Meunier. The grape gets its name from the white flour-like powdery speckles on its leaves, like those on the coat of a miller *(meunier)*.

© *Champagne Pammier*

The town of Epernay, the capital of *le champagne*, is an ideal centre for touring the region. Visitors seeking rest and relaxation will find a wide choice of fine hotels, restaurants and friendly *chambres d'hôtes* both in the centre and neighbouring villages.

Because of its proximity to Paris the valley of the Marne offers visitors a wide choice of activities, including boat trips on the river and fascinating châteaux to visit. There is even a hamlet which has an eco-museum and another with a snail farm – where you can sample the wares washed down with the farmer's own champagne.

From Château-Thierry to Epernay

Our route runs from west to east, from Paris to Châlons-en-Champagne with **Château-Thierry** as our first stop. If you're seeking refreshment in a serene setting then the restaurant of the 18-hole (72 par) golf course set in the aptly name **Val Secret** (secret valley), close to junction 20 of the motorway, is ideal. (Tel: 03 23 83 07 25)

Riddling at Champagne Pannier
© *Champagne Pannier*

The ancient once-fortified town is home to **Champagne Pannier**, founded in 1899 by Louis Eugène Pannier at Dizy, near Eperney.

First War Memorial, Dormas
© *CDT Champagne Ardenne*

It moved here in the 1930s when it took over two kilometres of galleries that had been dug out of the hillside a thousand years before by Thierry, the Count of Champagne, for limestone to build the fortified city that still bears his name.

In 1974 the ownership passed from the Pannier family to the farmers and became a co-operative. In 1998 it joined forces with two other *Caves Co-operative* – the *Union Auboise* from Bar-sur-Seine, who make Veuve A. Devaux, and COGEVI from Aÿ – to form *Alliance Champagne*.

An interesting visit with the opportunity of tasting some well-made, useful champagnes. 25, rue Roger-Catilion €. Monday to Friday 9am to 12 noon, and 2 to 6.30pm. (Tel: 03 26 69 51 30 E-mail: champagnepannier@champagnepannier.com)

Take the N3 and follow the winding river for some 24km and you come to **Dormans**. In the Parc du Château is the Memorial to the battle of the Marne, built on the orders of Marshal Foch to commemorates the two battles as well as the one and half million French soldiers killed during the Great War. Open all the year Monday and Wednesday to Saturday 2.30 to 6.30pm. And 10am to 12 noon, 2.30 to 6.30pm Sundays from April to early Nov. € for guided tour (in French).

About 2km beyond the town is the hamlet of **Try** and here you will find *L'Escargot de Champagne*. This is a snail farm and museum where you can see and sample this French delicacy accompanied by the owner. M. Moreau's, champagne. 8, rue des Plumons. € Only by appointment (Tel: 03 26 58 10 77)

Crossing the river at **Port Binson** you will see the monument to Pope Urban II, built in 1862 at **Châtillon-sur-Marne**. Born in Troyes, Urban raised the First Crusade in 1095. You can climb up the stairs inside the statue for a wonderful view across the valley and its vineyards.

Close by **Villers sur Châtillon** is a very pretty village which, each December, is illuminated with little lights. **Jacky Charpentier** is a grower with new cellars at the top of the village who has been practising eco-friendly viticulture for over ten years. They make excellent champagne and also have self-catering accommodation for four to six people. 88, rue de Reuil. € (Tel: 03 26 58 05 78 E-mail: champagnejcharpentier@wanadoo.fr)

Returning to the south bank and the once fortified village of **Oeuilly**, you will find a fascinating eco-museum of three buildings preserved as they were in the early 1900s. It comprises a peasant's home dating from 1642 saved as it was around 1914 and the village school from 1900 where you can take dictation with a steel pen and ink at a desk. And finally there is the village distillery with a still dating from 1850 – do look at the photographs, particularly those of the growers revolution in 1911 – with a cooperage museum on the first floor. Allow a good couple of hours. € Open May to Nov. every day except Tuesdays, 2 to 6pm. (Tel: 03 26 57 10 30)

Two generations of Tarlants in the vineyard
© Champagne Tarlant

At the top of the village is Champagne **Tarlant**, an outstanding winegrower with 13ha of vineyards. Jean-Mary Tarlant and his son Benoît (excellent English) continue a family tradition that dates back to 1787. Today they are among the most innovative of growers, maturing most of their base wines in oak barrels and producing some fascinating light *dosage* champagnes including a Brut-Zero. Every Saturday, from March till December, Benoît conducts an all-day session explaining what is happening in the vineyard and the winery; advance booking essential. For example visit them in April and you'll learn about blending while in June you'll discover all about the vine and its environment.

The family has converted the accommodation that originally housed the pickers at harvest time into a well-equipped *chambre d'hôte*, serving breakfast in summer on a new terrace. (Tel: 03 26 58 30 60 E-mail: champagne@tarlant.com)

And on along the Marne to Epernay, that is unless you take the alternative route along the beautiful valley of the river Surmelin.

If the latter then leave the N3 at Fossoy, 9km from Château-Thierry, turning left on to the D4 towards **Condé-en-Brie** (6.5km). In summer visit the very handsome Château de Condé that is open every afternoon throughout June, July and August. (Tel: 03 26 53 35 86) Web-site: www.chateaudeconde.com

Continue along the D4 for around 7km to **Le Breuil** and **Jean Moutardier**, a modestly-sized producer that traces its lineage back to 1650. This merchant house with a growing reputation in the UK is run by an Englishman, Jonathan Saxby, who married M. Moutardier's daughter, Elizabeth, who is a wine-broker.

Château Montmort-Lucy
© *CDT Champagne Ardenne*

Jonathan enjoys showing British visitors around the winery and explaining the intricacies of champagne production in easy-to-understand English. His expressive champagnes include a 100% Pinot Meunier. Open all the year during office hours, Monday to Friday, but closed the last two weeks in August. (Tel: 03 26 38 50 73 E-mail: moutardi@ebc.net)

And so back on the road to **Orbais** (7km) then left to **Mareuil-en-Brie** (3km) and right to **Montmort-Lucy** (6km) and the spectacular renaissance Château de Montmort set in a huge park. The home of the de Montmort family since 1074, it stands proud of the village high on its 14m platform and is entered by a drawbridge which is still raised every evening. It has a most singular internal ramp set in a tower to enable horses to get up and down under cover. Don't miss the splendid small museum in the stables which tells the story of the local Resistance during the 1939-45 war. Guided visits Monday to Friday between 15th July and 15th Sept., Saturday by appointment only. (Tel: 03 2659 21 09 E-mail: hubertremond@aol.com)

The village inn *Le Cheval Blanc* (White Horse), run by the Cousinart family, is comfortable with well-equipped rooms and a reliable restaurant. (Tel: 03 26 5910 03)

Gérard Thiroux, chef-patron at the *Hôtel-Restaurant de la Place* serves traditional regional dishes. 3 Pl. du Général de Gaulle. (Tel: 03 26 59 10 38)

The North Bank – Damery to Epernay

Damery is an important champagne centre. Almost every other house contains a champagne producer. There are two that are of particular interest, Jeepers and Lenoble.

The Goutrobes have lived in Damery since around 1790 and with three families of the same name offering their champagnes in the same street – rue Georges Clemenceau – it was obvious that at least one of them should call theirs something different. In 1944 Armand Goutroube returned from the war handicapped and the government allowed him to buy a Jeep to enable him to get among his vines. So he named his brand **Jeepers**. Today proud owners of Jeeps old and new descend upon Damery to visit Armand's son Christian, returning home with cases of his ultra-clean champagne. Visitors welcome during the week between 9am and 12 noon and 2 to 5.30pm (Tel: 03 26 58 65 67)

© Champagne Charles Heidsieck

A.R Lenoble is a low profile, high reputation producer. The champagne house, founded by Armand Raphaël Graser, is run today by his great-grandchildren, brother and sister Antoine and Anne Malassagne. The initials A.R. are after the founder and the name Lenoble because he believed that champagne was the noblest of all wines: you can't fault that! All the base wines are made in part using new French oak barrels. The Lenoble style has been described as 'ripe, creamy, rich and full of fruit'. It is certainly an easy drinking, anytime wine that has become the house champagne of numerous leading British restaurants. Visits Monday to Friday, but only by appointment. Excellent English. 35-37 rue Douce. (Tel: 03 26 58 42 60 E-mail: contact@champagne-lenoble.com)

Leave Damery by the D1 in the direction **Cumières**. Just beyond the town at the hamlet of **l'Echelle Reuil** there is a brand new and very well equipped *chambre d'hôte*, **Domaine Bacchus**, run by a young couple, M. & Mme. Arnaud Billard and their helpful children. He is a grape farmer and a member of a local co-operative. The large, airy rooms have excellent showers and some look out over the valley to tree-lined hills the other side of the river. The not-to-be-missed secret of this particular *chambre d'hôte* lies in the basement. It is a charming 75m² **model of a champagne village** at the beginning of the last century. Children and grown-ups are enchanted by the display which includes a number of animated features. The model village € is open every day except Wednesday from 9 to 11am and 1.30 to 5pm; the admission price includes a glass of M. Billard's champagne for the adults. (Tel: 03 26 58 66 60 E-mail: info@domaine-bacchus.com)

Continue down the road to the village of **Cumières**. Among the many producers based here is the old-established family merchant house of **René Geoffroy** who has owned vineyards in the village since the 17th century. Jean-Baptiste Geoffroy's champagnes, made without a malolactic transformation, are soft

© CDT Champagne Ardenne

and smooth with very fine flavours. He also makes some excellent still *coteaux champanois*. Appointment preferred, Monday to Saturday 9am to 12 noon and 2 to 5.30pm. 150, rue du Bois-des-Jots (Tel: 03 26 55 32 31 E-mail: info@champagne-geoffroy.com)

'Serious' is the best way to describe Jean-Claude Rambach's restaurant *Le Caveau* in the rue de la Coopérative, off the main Damery-Dizy road. Built into the side of the hill, this friendly mid-priced restaurant is always full of *champenois* who enjoy its excellent food and relaxing atmosphere. (Tel: 03 26 54 83 23 E-mail: jc-rambch@restaurant-le-caveau.com)
Website: www.restaurant-le-caveau.com

How about a lunch cruise up the Marne? A stern-wheeler river-boat leaves each day at 12 noon from the quay beside the bridge at Cumières and returns at 3pm, Plenty of parking space. (Tel: 03 26 54 49 51 E-mail: croisi.champagne@wanadoo.fr)

Epernay

*Napoleon looked awfully cute
With his hand stuck into his suit.
His favourite Champagne,
Please let me explain,
Was Moët's Imperial Brut.*

Epernay, with its 100km of champagne cellars, *is* champagne; everything else comes a distant second. Visitors flock to visit the big houses, relax in its hotels and sip champagne in its numerous bars and restaurants. The town's centre, the Place de la République, lies at the start of the wonderfully named

Place de la République
© *OT Epernay*

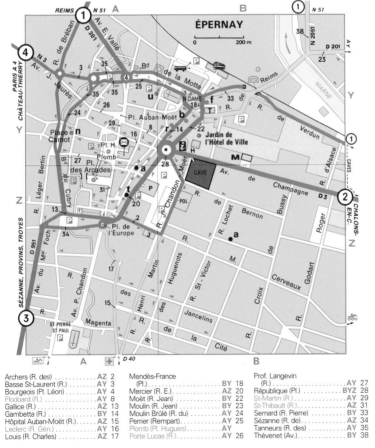

ÉPERNAY

© *Authorisation No. 0411449*

Avenue de Champagne which Winston Churchill called the finest address in Europe. The Avenue begins and ends with two giant champagne houses – Moët & Chandon and Mercier – with names like Besserat de Bellefon, Boizel, Perrier-Jouët and Pol Roger spread along its noble length.

So let's start with the bottom of the Avenue with the biggest champagne producer of them all, **Moët & Chandon**. Moët is understandably the most popular visit of them all and among the best organised.

The house was founded in 1683 by Claude de Moët but it was his grandson Jean-Rémy's friendship with Napoleon Bonaparte – to whom he dedicated his *Brut Impérial* – that put the house on the map, from where it has never disappeared. At the turn of the 19th century Jean-Rémy built two identical mansions on the other side of the road. One was for his family and the other, *La Résidence Trianon*, for Napoleon and his entourage when the Emperor travelled to the east.

Pol Roger's majestic headquarters
© *Champagne Pol Roger*

What is remarkable about Moët, which sells some 24 million bottles a year, is that it manages to retain quality and consistency. Visits each day from 8th March to 11th November, 9.30 to 11.30am and 2 to 4.30pm. Closed weekends from 12th November to 7th March. 20, Avenue de Champagne. The cost depends upon the number of wines to be tasted. (Tel: 03 26 51 20 20 E-mail: visites@moet.tm.fr)

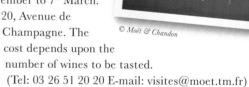

© *Moët & Chandon*

Mercier, at the top of the hill, is also part of the giant Moët-Hennessy empire. It was founded in 1858 by Eugène Mercier who would stop at nothing to promote his wines. He had a huge oak cask made, some 1,000 times bigger than the traditional 220 litre barrel, and had 24 white oxen haul it to Paris for the 1889 Exhibition. On 10th September 1891 the French President, Sadi Carnot, was driven through Mercier's cellars in

Eugène Mercier's giant barrel for the 1889 Paris Exhibition
© *Champagne Mercier*

an open carriage drawn by four white horses. Mercier does have an unusual champagne in its range; a romantic demi-sec rosé that is ideal for weddings. Try it if you can. Today Mercier still delights in the unusual and visitors descend by lift and are taken around part of the 18km of cellars by train. € Visits each day from 9.30 to 11.30am and 2 to 4.30-5pm at weekends, March to Dec. (Tel: 03 26 51 22 21)

Half way up the Avenue is Champagne **Perrier-Jouët**; again the 't' is pronounced. A noble house dating back to 1811 and closely associated with the *Belle Epoque*. P-J, as it is known to its friends, provides stylish visits on a much more human scale and an

The Art Nouveau Salon
© CDT Perrier-Jouët

opportunity to admire the early 20th century décor of their Art Nouveau salon with works by Daum, Galle – whose floral arabesque decorates their *fin du siècle cuvée prestige* bottle – Guimard, Lalique, Majorelle and Rodin. 26, Av. de Champagne. € Open Monday to Friday 9 to 11.15am and 2 to 4.15pm.

Perrier-Jouët, now owned by Allied-Domecq, offers four different styles of visit including a half day in the vineyards, which must be booked in advance, as must visits to *la Maison Belle Epoque*. (Tel: 03 26 53 38 10 E-mail: frederique_baveret@perrier-jouet.fr)

Sir Winston Churchill called No. 44 Avenue de Champagne, the home of **Pol Roger**, 'The most drinkable address in Europe.' It was in 1848 that Pol – *patois* or local slang for Paul – Roger began making champagne. The Roger family soon added his forename to their surname and called themselves Pol-Roger while the company name has no hyphen and remains Pol Roger et Cie. Predominantly Chardonnay, Pol Roger wines achieve a deliciously light citrus finish. It is an apéritif style much admired by champagne *cognoscenti* all over the world who enthuse about the creamy mousse and the tiny pinprick bubbles.

In 1944 Sir Winston Churchill was lunching at the British Embassy in Paris which had just been re-opened after the war by the Duff Coopers. Among the guests was Madame Odette Pol-Roger who, like Sir Winston, was a great patriot and fighter. Throughout the German occupation this elegant lady – known to all as *Tante Odette* – had planted her garden with red, white and blue flowers and invariably wore a diamond RAF brooch. She and 'Winnie' struck up

Winston Churchill & Odette Pol-Roger at the races
© Champagne Pol Roger

© Champagne de Castellane

a friendship that lasted through his life. Sir Winston named one of his racehorses after the champagne that he always insisted on being served. When Pol Roger won the Coronation Stakes at Sandown Park in Coronation year, Epernay went wild and much Pol Roger was drunk that night on both sides of the Channel.

After his death in 1965 Pol Roger went into mourning and added a black line around its labels. The house also created its most prestigious *cuvée* – Sir Winston Churchill – which is only made in the most outstanding years and was, for a long time, only available in the UK and then the USA. Although the family refuse to divulge the blend it is certainly packed with *Grand Cru* Pinot Noir from very fine vineyards.

The Epernay skyline is dominated by a giant water tower that proudly proclaims **De Castellane**. This champagne house was founded in 1890 by the Vicomte Florens de Castellane who used as his label the red cross of St André, the standard of the oldest regiment in Champagne. A member of the Laurent-Perrier group that also owns Salon – the most exclusive of all champagnes – De Castellane is a brand very much on its way up. The wines, which improve each year, are delightfully refreshing with excellent structure, fruit and length.

Don't be put off by the size of the premises. The visit is certainly interesting while the view from the 60m tower, with its 237 steps, is well worth the climb. The tour includes a collection of old printing presses used to produce bottle labels as well as the most comprehensive collection of champagne labels anywhere. € Visits Monday to Friday, normal office hours. (Tel: 03 26 51 19 19)

If you can find your way to 67 rue Chaude-Ruelle your could be in for a surprise. The old established merchant house of **Leclerc-Briant**, dating back to 1664, offers an opportunity of abseiling down to the cellar at the end of a rope! But most people just take the stairs down and the goods lift back!

Pascal Leclerc is in the process of changing his 30ha of vineyards over to organic viticulture which means that he no longer uses toxic pesticides or petrochemical fertilisers. Instead he is employing eco-friendly natural materials that, while they may reduce the yield at harvest time, improve the quality and character of the juice.

Abseiling down to the cellar
© Champagne Leclerc-Briant

Pascal has something of a reputation for being different in other ways. His *Rubis Rosé de Noirs* for example, made from 100% Pinot Noir, is so dark that it is virtually a sparkling red wine. However, his *Cuvée Divine*, made from equal parts Chardonnay and Pinot Noir, is both accessible and succulent. € Visits Monday to Friday during office hours. Appointments preferred. (Tel: 03 26 54 49)

Alfred Gratien is a most unusual champagne house in a number of ways. M. Gratien came from the Loire Valley and started to make sparkling wine at Saumur (Gratien & Meyer) before establishing his champagne house in Epernay the same year – 1864. A most traditional house, they buy in all their juice and make their base wine in small oak barrels. The *chef-de-cave*, Jean-Pierre Jaeger, is the third generation of his family to hold this key position and the champagnes they have produced over the years have always proved extremely popular with The Wine Society which they have been supplying continuously since 1907. Their complex, yet always refreshing wines, have those Anglo-Saxon yeasty, biscuity aromas. Their vintage *Cuvée-Paradis* (paradise) is delightful when young, then goes to sleep for a number of years, awaking with mellow and toasty aromas. In 2002 the family sold the business to the German *sekt* company of Henkell who wisely do not plan any changes here at all. 30, rue Maurice Cerveaux. Visits by appointment only. (Tel: 03 26 54 38 20)

Château de Saran
© *Moët & Chandon*

© *Moët & Chandon*

Just beyond the town, going east on the main N3 to Paris, is the village of Mardeuil where you will find an interesting small co-operative, **Beaumont des Crayères**. With some 210 members who between them only own 80ha, they are little more than weekend gardeners; yet winemaker Jean-Paul Bertus constantly makes champagnes bursting with richness. Visits during office hours Monday to Friday, appointments not always necessary. 64, rue de la Liberté. (Tel: 03 26 55 29 40)

It would also be wrong to leave Epernay without mentioning **Marne & Champagne**. This massive champagne complex, second in size only to Moët, buys some 24% of all the grapes sold on the open market, producing prodigious quantities of own label champagnes. Established in 1930 by Gaston Burtin, it is now

© OT Epernay

© OT Epernay

owned by his niece, Mme. Marie-Laurence Mora and her husband, and also owns Gauthier, Besserat de Bellefon and Lanson which has its own production facility in Reims.

If you have a sweet tooth, then visit the **La Chocolaterie Thibaut** on the supermarket site by the roundabout on the way to Pierry. This family enterprise specialises in making the chocolate champagne corks filled with *Marc de Champagne*, one of the region's specialities. They will show you how they take liquid chocolate, made from cocoa butter, and form the corks that are then filled with the local brandy. As well as champagne corks they also make chocolate rabbits, cats and dogs and a whole host of other delicious shapes. You will have plenty of ideas for presents, if you have a way of keeping the chocolate chilled on your return journey. Allow 45 minutes for the visit € which take place between 9am and 12 noon and 2 and 7pm Monday to Saturday between Easter and 10th Dec. (Tel: 02 26 51 58 04)

Tired of walking? Then why not let the train take the strain. A little road train runs around the streets of Epernay from 1st May to the 31st October. The total journey is just under an hour and trains leave the Avenue de Champagne every Tuesday to Sunday at 10 and 11am and then every hour from 1.30 to 5.30pm.

If you would love to go up into the hills to see some of the vineyards but don't fancy driving, then telephone Mme. Nathalie Domi of **Champagne Domi Moreau**. The charming English-speaking guide will pick you up at your hotel or *chambre d'hôte* for a half-day tour of the vineyards. She will drive you around the hills explaining exactly what is going on in the vineyards. She might even get you trying your hand at it! She then takes you back to her family winery in Mancy where her husband will show you the whole complex process that creates champagne before tasting some of his own refreshing wines. Champagne Domi Moreau, 14 rue du Bas, Mancy. (Tel: 03 26 59 72 72)

At midday in Epernay, like the rest of France, everything stops between noon and 2pm so why not do the same and enjoy a leisurely meal? The **Cave à Champagne** (The Champagne Cellar) 16 rue Gambetta – runs between Pl. de la République and Pl.

Mendes-France and the station – is popular with local businessmen. Chef-patron Bernard Ocio offers simple menus and an excellent selection of growers' champagnes. Closed Tuesday night and Wednesday. (Tel: 03 26 55 50 70)

Table Kobus, 3 rue Dr. Rousseau-behind the large church to the west of Pl. Mendes-France – is a stylish brasserie with a hint of *la Belle Epoque* where many champagne producers entertain their customers. The menu is expansive without being over-expensive. Booking essential at weekends. Closed most of August, Monday, Sunday and Thursday nights. (Tel: 03 26 51 53 53)

If you want to lunch with the champagne producers than you should go the **Le 7 des Berceaux**, the wine bar at the Hotel Berceaux, 13 rue Berceaux – this runs parallel and behind the rue Mercier, south from the Pl. de la République. The simple menu comes from the same kitchens that serve the hotel's highly-rated restaurant and there is a wide range of champagnes and still wines at sensible prices, many by the glass and half bottle. Closed weekends. (Tel: 03 26 55 28 84)

However, if you only feel like a snack then try the terrace of **La Progress** in Pl. de la République. Nothing elaborate, a salad or Croque-Monsieur (ham and cheese on toast), a half-bottle of champagne, fruit juice or a *pression*, draught beer. (Tel: 03 26 55 22 72)

For a restful dinner go to **Bacchus Gourmet**, 21 rue Gambetta – almost opposite le Cave à Champagne. This small restaurant knows how to look after guests who enjoy fine food and wines in a simple yet smart setting. Closed Monday and Tuesday. (Tel: 03 26 51 11 44)

Les Cépages (The grape varieties) 16 rue Fauvette – near Pl. Carnot to the west of the town – offers classic French cooking with choice champagnes surrounded by paintings by regional artists. No smoking. Closed most of July, Wednesday and Thursday. (Tel: 03 26 55 16 95)

© *Huyghens Danrgal/Collection C.I.V.C*

Or return to **Les Berceaux** and experience M. Michelon's exquisite cooking in his hotel's elegant restaurant. He might even join you after dinner over a fine Havana cigar and an excellent cognac. And why not stay the night under his roof? The modest rooms are less luxurious than the restaurant. No car parking. (Tel: 03 26 55 28 84 E-mail: lesberceaux@wanadoo.fr)

Clos Raymi, 3 rue Joseph Venoge – behind Moët & Chandon – is a small luxurious hotel with seven splendidly appointed rooms owned by the mother-in-law of Anselme Selosse, one of champagne's leading bio-dynamic producers. Car parking. No restaurant or lift. Breakfast in the garden in summer. More like staying in a private house than an hotel. (Tel: 03 26 51 00 58 E-mail: closraymi@wanadoo.fr)

© Hote Royal Champagne, Champillon

Hotel Champagne, 50 rue Eugène Mercier-south of the Pl. de la République-is a centrally located practical commercial hotel. No car parking. No restaurant. (Tel: 03 26 53 10 60 E-mail: infos@bw-hotel-champagne.com)

Just beyond Epernay on the way south and east is the village of Monthelon. Here André and Martine Pienne run **Les Cépages**, a small, simple but spotlessly clean *chambre d'hôte*. You will certainly be offered a glass of André's champagne in the sitting room before you go out to dinner and next morning you will breakfast around the kitchen table. 38 rue Gaston Poittevin. (Tel: 03 26 59 74 63)

Also beyond the town are two luxurious hotels, both with Michelin starred restaurants.

The Royal Champagne, at **Champillon** to the north of the town on the way to Reims, is an old posting house. The lavishly appointed rooms are set outside the main building and overlook vineyards. The hotel is most convenient for the village of Hautvillers. Michelin starred restaurant.

Hostellerie La Briqueterie
© Hostellerie La Briqueterie

(Tel: 03 26 52 87 11 E-mail: royalchampagne@wanadoo.fr)

Hostellerie La Briqueterie (the brickyard) is a modern hotel at **Vinay**, to the south of the town off the road to Sezanne. Set in a garden with an indoor swimming pool, sauna and gym. Michelin starred restaurant. (Tel: 03 26 59 99 99 E-mail: info@labriqueterie.com)

Hautvillers

The village of **Hautvillers** lies 7km to the north and west of Epernay in the regional nature reserve of the Mountain of Reims. If Epernay is the capital of champagne, then Hautvillers is its birthplace or *berceau*. It was here at the abbey, behind the church with its pepper-pot tower, that Dom Pérignon lived and worked as cellar master for 47 years between 1668 and 1715. The abbey is now owned by Moët & Chandon and unfortunately is not open to the public.

Allow a couple of hours to walk around this pretty unspoilt village and don't forget your camera. Park your car and pick up a plan of the village from the tourist office in the Pl. de la République and stroll along the lanes looking up at the wrought iron signs set above the entrances of many homes. They were the idea of Jean Couten who was mayor of Hautvillers during the 1950s. Each sign represents the family and their trade. The best known and most photographed of these signs is in rue Hubarde and shows the various steps in the production of champagne.

© OT Hautvillers

The village church, where Dom Pérignon is buried close to the altar, is rich in history. Opposite the church are the cellars of **Champagne Jean-Marie Gobillard & Fils**. Their Grande Réserve is specially commended. Visits by appointment, but it would be nice to return home with at least one bottle from Dom Pérignon's village. (Tel: 03 26 51 00 24)

Return to the Pl. de la République for a well-earned *flûte de champagne*.

© OT Hautvillers

Dizy to Châlons-en-Champagne

This section of the route runs for some 30km along the north bank of the river Marne. Leave Epernay towards Reims and the N51, cross over the river Marne and turn right towards **Aÿ** and you are already in **Dizy**. This tiny village is packed with champagne producers but there are perhaps two that you should consider visiting-both only by appointment.

Jacquesson & Fils was founded in 1798 by Claude Jacquesson. In 1810 Napoleon visited their cellars and presented the family with a gold medal for their champagnes. The Krug family worked here to learn their trade. The house, run since 1974 by the Chiquet family, produces beautifully balanced and expressive wines. The non-vintage champagnes are made in part from reserve wines stored in large oak tuns. 65, rue du Colonel Fabien. € By appointment, Monday to Friday, office hours. (Tel: 03 26 55 68 11)

Another part of the Chiquet family is **Gaston Chiquet** who are an important family of winegrowers producing excellent champagnes. Nicolas Chiquet planted his first vines in 1746 and since then eight generations have carried on the family tradition. They began selling their own champagne in 1935 and have 22ha under vine, with an average age of 35 years, in some 40 parcels of land. The business is run by Claude Chiquet and his sons Antoine and Nicolas. They follow traditional methods and, by maturing their wines for as many years as they feel necessary, have built up a reputation for champagnes of considerable finesse. In 1935 the family planted Chardonnay in their vineyards at Aÿ, best known for its Pinot Noir, and now make an excellent *Blanc de Blancs* from these grapes which, after three years maturing in their cellars, is round, full and deliciously fresh. 912, Avenue du Général Leclerc. € Appointment not always necessary, Monday to Friday. (Tel: 03 26 55 22 02)

Driving east you are almost immediately in **Aÿ** (pronounced Eye-E), the centre for Pinot Noir. This small town is home to a number of famous producers like Bollinger, Deutz and Gosset, as well as a winegrower with a difference – **Henri Goutorbe**.

They are not only the largest, and arguably the best, winegrower in Aÿ, they are also one of the region's leading nurserymen selling vines. The business was founded in 1945 by Emile Goutorbe who had been cellar-master at Perrier-Jouët. Today it is run by his son Henri and his grandson René and their wives. Their splendid 17th century premises and cellars are in the middle of Aÿ. The family's 20ha of vineyards have an average age of 25 years. They make a range of five champagnes that are given a malolactic conversion. They also produce a *Ratafia de Champagne* as well as two brandies, a *Vieille Fine de la Marne* and a *Vieux Marc de Champagne* made for them by the local distillery from the residue left over from their pressing and the deposits from the bottom of the vats. 9 bis, rue Jeanson, € Visits Monday to Saturday 9am to 12 noon and 2 to 5pm. (Tel: 03 26 55 21 70)

Madame Béatrice Cointreau
© Champagne Gosset

Established in 1584, **Gosset** is undoubtedly the oldest wine house in the whole of champagne, only it didn't start making sparkling wines until very much later. The house remained in the Gosset family for 409 years and was acquired in 1993 by Renaud

Cointreau who also own Cognac Frapin. Today the business is run by Béatrice Cointreau who works tirelessly to preserve its reputation for top quality wines, made without the malo' and with some wood. The delicate salmon-pink *Célebris* rosé, shot through with tiny bubbles, has elegant floral and red-fruit notes. 69, rue Jules-Blondeau. Tastings only and always by appointment. (Tel: 03 26 56 99 56 E-mail: info@champagne-gosset.com)

Aÿ is also home to the region's main distillery, **Jean Goyard et Cie**, a family firm that produces almost all of the *Marc* and *Fine de Champagne*. Their brandies are especially delicate and aromatic because the *Marc* is made from the residue of grapes that have only been lightly pressed while the *Fine* is mostly made from the wine rich sediment that pops out of the bottle when it is disgorged.

When it comes to food, then enjoy the rustic interior of the ***Vieux Puits*** (Old Wells) where you will find reliable regional cooking and, of course, excellent champagnes. 18 rue Roger Sondag. Closed Wednesday and Thursday. (Tel: 03 26 56 96 53)

Why not stay the night at a *chambre d'hôte* in the centre of the town, by the church, run by the family of one of Aÿ's leading wine farmers, **Roger Brun**. Philippe and Sophie Brun will welcome you to converted grape-pickers' lodgings, close to their cellars, and enjoy tasting their wines with you. The *Brun* rosé is legendary while their nv prestige *Cuvée des Sires*, made from 98% Aÿ Pinot Noir and two percent Chardonnay is an absolute joy! Excellent English, you might even get your copy of The Times with your morning breakfast! (Tel: 03 26 54 56 37)

Aÿ is home to **Bollinger** whose champagnes are every bit as elegant as their beautiful mansion at 16 rue Jules Lobet which opens up at the back on to their own vineyards. Unfortunately they are not able to receive casual visitors. The founder – a German, Jacques Bollinger – married the daughter of a major Aÿ landowner, Admiral Comte Emmanuel de Villemont, and opened his champagne business in 1829. The elegant Bollinger style is set by the quality of all of its wines, many of which are fermented in oak barrels while the reserve wines are kept in magnums sealed with real corks. Bollinger's great

The house of Bollinger
© *Champagne Bollinger*

wine is their *Blanc de Noirs Vieilles Vignes Françaises*, only made in exceptional years from vertically trained Pinot Noir vines in Aÿ and Bouzy.

The next village is **Mareuil-sur-Aÿ**. Champagne Roger **Pouillon & Fils** are on the right, just before you enter the town. Fabrice Pouillon is one of the new young winegrowers who, while respecting tradition, concentrates exclusively on achieving quality. Although he only has 6.5ha of vineyards, these cover 25 parcels in six different villages and provide him with a broad range of flavours and aromas to blend together to create his eight champagnes. 3, Chemin de la Couple. € Appointment not always necessary. (Tel: 03 26 52 60 08)

© *Champagne Billecart-Salmon*

Billecart-Salmon is one of the greatest champagnes produced today. This small family house constantly achieves superb quality with exceptional finesse. Francis Roland-Billecart is the fifth generation of his family producing classic, refreshing champagnes that can be found at most of the world's great restaurants. Francis has begun to make a most exclusive *Blanc de Noirs* from Pinot Noir vines planted in a tiny enclosed vineyard alongside the winery. Appointment essential. 40, rue Carnot. (Tel: 03 26 52 60 22
E-mail: billecart@champagne-billecart.fr)

© *Champagne Billecart-Salmon*

The House of **Philipponnat** no longer receives visitors. However as you leave the town you will pass by the jewel in its crown; the Clos des Goisses, a single enclosed 5ha vineyard that slopes to the south east, producing exceptional high quality grapes. The slope of the hill, reflected in the river Marne, looks like a champagne bottle. The wine, made from a blend of 70% Pinot Noir and 30% Chardonnay, has a singular ability to age for 15 to 20 years!

Domaine de la Marotière, down beside the canal, is an old town house set in a splendid garden that offers outstanding *chambre d'hôte* accommodation and an exceptional dinner that has to be booked in advance. Yves Giraud, an excellent cook and a most valuable source of local information, can be relied upon to find some interesting wines as well as unusual *digestifs* to follow the meal. Domaine de la Marotière 11, rue Sadi Carnot. Car parking. (Tel: 03 26 52 11 00 E-mail: lamarotiere@wanadoo.fr).

Our next stopping place is the little town of **Tours sur Marne** and that means **Laurent-Perrier**. Modern and superbly equipped, Laurent-Perrier is one of the few still-independent giants of the champagne industry. The house was established at Tours-sur-Marne in 1812 by Eugène Laurent. When he died in 1886 his widow, Mathilde Perrier, took over and added her name to the business.

© *Champagne Laurent-Perrier*

In 1938 the house passed to the Nonancourt family who still own it today, together with four other well-known champagne houses – de Castellane, Delamotte and Salon. Laurent-Perrier's great strength is the depth of styles that it creates enabling it to match both the mood and the fickle fashion of international markets. This approach has enabled the company to become the fifth largest champagne house in the world. Laurent-Perrier claims to be the first champagne producer to introduce stainless steel fermentation vats; it also sets the pace for pink champagne with its 100% Pinot Noir wine made from a macerated pink base. But its greatest champagne is *Grand Siècle*, *La Cuvée*, a blend of exclusively *grand cru* grapes from two, three or more vintage years. Peerless blending makes it one of the most outstanding of all the *Cuvées Prestiges*. Open Monday to Friday, € visits by appointment only. (Tel: 03 26 58 91)

The ***Touraine Champenosie*** is a charming canal-side inn with an excellent rustic restaurant which has been owned and run by the same family since 1907. Simple but adequate rooms (the author often stays here). In summer the rooms at the back are quieter. Car parking. Excellent breakfasts. Closed Thursday. Rue Magasin. (Tel: 03 26 58 91 93)

And so on to ***Châlons-en-Champagne*** which was, until quite recently, known as Châlons sur Marne. This tranquil and picturesque small city, built on river and canal, is in fact the administrative capital of the Department of the Marne.

Joseph Perrier was established in Châlons in 1825 and today still retains its 19th century charm. Its 3km of cellars are dug into the side of the hill so there are no long flights of steep steps to climb up and down. The well-blended classical champagnes range from

a refreshing apéritif style to some deeper, rounder *cuvées* that are delicious with fish. Today the House belongs to Alain Thiènot but is still run by Jean-Claude Fourmon, a descendant of Paul Pithois who acquired the business from the Perrier family in 1888. The wines are made by Claude Dervin, the third generation of his family to be cellar-master here. 69, Ave. de Paris. € Appointment essential. (Tel: 03 26 70 57 16
E-mail: Josephperrier@wanadoo.fr)

A city on a more human scale, there is plenty to see in Châlons-en-Champagne, with its stone and half-timbered houses, and few better ways of doing so than by boat. In the high season there are daily 30-minute boat trips on the Mau and Nau canals from 2.30 to 6.30pm from the Quai des Arts, beside the Tourist Office.

Au Carillon Gourmand is a modest restaurant that in summer spreads on to the pavement and whose menu is largely set by whatever is fresh in the market that morning. 15b Pl. Mgr. Tissier, opposite Notre-Dame-en-Vaux church. Closed most of August, Wednesday, Sunday night. (Tel: 03 26 64 45 07)

Pré St-Alpin is a smart traditional restaurant in an elegant 1900 *fin de siècle* setting. Closed Sunday night. 2b rue Abbé, top of Pl. République. (Tel: 03 26 70 20 26)

Hotel Renard is certainly original with its idiosyncratic, modern, well-equipped rooms and interior patio garden. Central location close to the shops. 24, Pl. République.
(Tel: 03 26 68 0378 E-mail: lerenard51@wanadoo.fr)

The luxury hotel **Angleterre** is also in the centre of town. The comfortable well-appointed bedrooms, many with marble bathrooms, are complemented by Jacky Michel's superb Michelin-starred restaurant that attracts gourmets from all over the region. 19 Pl. Mgr. Tissier. (Tel: 03 26 68 21 51
E-mail: hot.angleterre@wanadoo.fr)

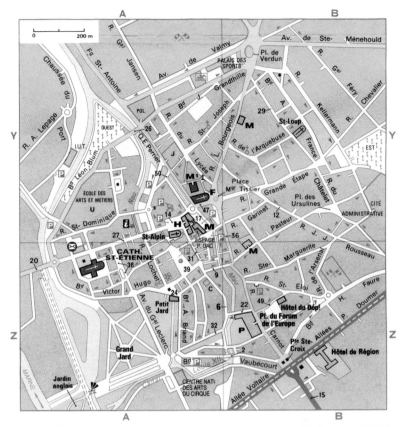

© *Authorisation No. 0411449*

CHÂLONS-EN-CHAMPAGNE

© *CDT Champagne Ardenne*

The Montagnes de Reims

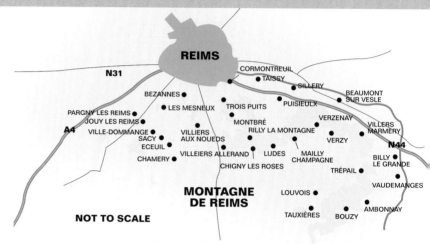

REIMS

CORMONTREUIL
TAISSY
SILLERY
BEZANNES
PUISIEULX
BEAUMONT
SUR VESLE
N31
TROIS PUITS
LES MESNEUX
PARGNY LES REIMS
JOUY LES REIMS
VERZENAY
VILLERS
MARMERY
MONTBRÉ
A4
VILLE-DOMMANGE
RILLY LA MONTAGNE
VILLIERS
SACY
AUX NOUEDS
VERZY
ECEUIL
N44
VILLEIERS ALLERAND
LUDES
MAILLY
CHAMERY
CHAMPAGNE
BILLY
LE GRANDE
CHIGNY LES ROSES
TRÉPAIL

VAUDEMANGES
**MONTAGNE
DE REIMS**
LOUVOIS
AMBONNAY
NOT TO SCALE
TAUXIÉRES
BOUZY

More of a hilly ridge than a mountain, nevertheless because of its *terroir* the Montagnes de Reims is a major source of exceptional champagnes. The vineyards are planted like a string of pearls from Chamery and Ecueil, south and west of Reims, along the north-facing slopes to Verzenay-with perhaps the most photographed windmill in France – and round the east slopes to south-facing Ambonnay and Bouzy.

During the First World War the eastern end of the mountain overlooked the German front line which went along where the autoroute and new TGV railway now run. The windmill was then an important observation post.

Not all the top growths are on the mountain. Some fine champagnes come from the villages of Merfy and Tigny to the west of Reims in what are sometimes referred to as *le petit montagne*. Fans of John Galsworthy's *Forsyte Saga* may recall old Swithin Forsyte's enthusiasm for his Sillery. This is one of the original *Grand Cru* villages and lies on the plain almost on the eastern edge of Reims.

The mountain is a national park with much to see and do; for example the strange dwarf beech tree of Verzy and the woodcutter's house at Germaine that shows what a forester's life was like in the olden days. Sept-Saulx, to the east, has a splendid nature park with plenty to entertain children of all ages; or just relax among the flowers and bird life or take a row around the lake.

The City of Reims

A city full of romance,
The French pronounce it as Rantz.
The British it seems
Prefer saying Reams,
Arriving in vast charabancs.

One of north Europe's most popular weekend destinations Reims – pronounced as if the 'm' was a double 'n', 'Rantz' – is a city that is as effervescent as the champagne it produces. It owes its fame to the Romans who quarried the chalk to build it. Over the years these quarries have been linked together to form the miles of cellars where tens of millions of bottles of champagne rest, slowly maturing, on their sides.

© *Authorisation No. 0411449*

REIMS

Alsace-Lorraine (R. d')	CX 2
Anatole-France (Cours)	BY 3
Arbalète (R. de l')	BY 4
Boulard (R.)	BY 6
Boulingrin (Pl. du)	BX 7
Brébant (Av.)	AY 8
Buirette (R.)	AY 12
Cadran St-Pierre (R.)	BY 13
Carmes (R. des)	BZ 16
Carnégie (Pl.)	BY 17
Carnot (R.)	BY 19
Champagne (Av. de)	CZ 22
Chemin Vert (R. du)	CZ 23
Colbert (R.)	BXY 26
Desteuque (R. E.)	BY 31
Dieu-Lumière (R.)	CZ 32
Dr-Jacquin (R.)	BXY 33
Dr-Knoéri (Pl. du)	CX 34
Dr-Lemoine (R.)	BX 35
Droits-de-l'Homme (Pl. des)	CZ 37
Drouet d'Erlon (Pl.)	AY 38
Dubois (R. Th.)	AY 39
Etape (R. de l')	AY 40
Farman (Av. H.)	CZ 43
Foch (Bd)	ABX 46
Forum (Pl.)	BY 47
Gerbert (R.)	BCY 50
Gouraud (Pl. Gén.)	CZ 51
Grand-Cerf (R. du)	CZ 52
Herduin (R. Lt)	BY 53
Houzeau Muiron (R.)	CY 54
Jamot (R. Paul)	BY 56
J.-J.-Rousseau (R.)	BX 57
Jean-Jaurès (Av.)	BCX
Lambert (Bd Victor)	CZ 58
Langlet (Crs J.-B.)	BY 59
Laon (Av. de)	ABX
Leclerc (Bd Général)	AY 60
Lefèbvre (R. E.)	CX 61
Louvois (R. de)	BZ 62
Magdeleine (R.)	AY 63
Martyrs-de-la-Résistance (Pl. des)	BY 65
Montlaurent (R.)	CY 67
Myron-Herrick (Pl.)	BY 68
Philipe (R. Gérard)	CZ 70
Prés.-F.-Roosevelt (R.)	AX 72
République (Pl. de la)	BX 73
Rockefeller (R.)	BY 75
Salines (R. des)	CZ 80
Sarrail (R. Gén.)	BX 82
St-Nicaise (Pl.)	CZ 78
Strasbourg (R. de)	CX 84
Talleyrand (R. de)	ABY
Temple (R. du)	BX 85
Thillois (R. de)	AY 86
Université (R. de l')	BY 88
Vesle (R. de)	ABY
Victor-Hugo (Bd)	CZ 90
Zola (R. Emile)	AX 92
16°-et-22°-Dragons (R. des)	CY 94

Vaulted cellars from the old Abbey St. Niçaise, now house Taittinger champagne
© *Champagne Taittinger*

For almost 200 years Reims stood in the path of invading armies from the east. In 1814 the Russians occupied the city for 24 hours before Napoleon came to recapture it in his last successful military operation. In 1870 it was the base for the Prussian army on its way to Paris. It was on the front line during the first Great World War when it suffered much damage and was largely rebuilt in the *art-nouveau* style of the Nancy school. After the 1918 war some 315 architects opened offices in Reims to supervise the reconstruction. The city was occupied throughout World War II and, on 7th May 1945, the German forces signed the surrender document in General Eisenhower's headquarters in what is now the Technical College.

Today Reims, at the heart of the champagne trade, is a city that makes visitors really welcome. There is plenty to feed both the eyes and the mind. And when both these senses have been fully satisfied then there are scores of wonderful restaurants where you can relax and 'restore' yourself for more sightseeing and cellar visits. Or you can just sit sipping champagne at pavement cafés and watch the world go by. In high season a little road train takes visitors around the city from close by the Information Office, beside the cathedral.

It is a large city but your hotel will be able to provide you with a map showing the major champagne houses and other places of interest open to visitors. Like most cities, driving around isn't much fun and parking can be difficult. But there is the excellent *Citadine* bus service for which you can buy day passes, getting on and off where you please.

Champagne Houses to Visit

There is no shortage of champagne houses to visit, so why not start at Ruinart which is where the commercial history of champagne began? At the turn of the 18th century a young Benedictine monk and scholar from Reims, Dom Thierry Ruinart, was able to watch the fascinating experiments being carried out by his friend Dom Pierre Pérignon at the Abbey of Hautvillers. From him he learnt the skill of blending wines from different *cuvées* and how to create the second fermentation in the bottle. All of this he passed on to his nephew, Nicolas Ruinart, who was a successful draper in Reims.

We don't know the exact date when Nicolas Ruinart started his business but we do know that the first sales were dated 1st September 1729. Prefacing the entry in the company's sales ledger Nicolas wrote, *"In the name of God and of the Virgin Mary shall this book be commenced."*

It was Nicolas's son Claude who moved the business to its present site on the *Butte Saint Nicaise* – or the hillock of St-Niçaise – above ancient Roman chalk pits. These individual workings, among the most spectacular in the whole of Champagne, were linked together. This has created an impressive labyrinth, some 30m underground, where the temperature remains constant winter and summer.

Cellars at Champagne Ruinart
© *Champagne Ruinart*

Over the years the Ruinart family travelled widely, selling their Champagne in Russia – which was until 1917 the sparkling wine's largest single market – the UK and the United States. At the same time their devotion to France earned them great wealth and honours. Nicolas's grandson Iréné, was an astute politician. He was made a viscount by the short-reigned Charles X who was crowned in Reims cathedral on 29th May 1825. This was to be the last title granted by a French king. In July 1830, following rioting in the streets Charles, the last of the Bourbons, was forced to abdicate.

© *Champagne Pommery*

Since 1963 the House of Ruinart has been an autonomous part of the mighty Moët-Hennessy combine. Ruinart produces some 100,000 cases a year of elegant and light style champagnes. Their sophisticated structure is provided by Chardonnay from their own 15ha of vineyards in *the grand Cru* village of Sillery.

The 'R' de Ruinart range is vibrant, crisp and sinewy with a particularly refreshing, floral and citrus Blanc-de-Blancs. The prestige Dom Ruinart demonstrates extraordinary quality at realistic prices. Visits Monday to Friday, strictly by appointment. € 4, rue des Crayères. (Tel: 03 26 77 51 51 E-mail: jpmoulin@ruinart.com)

Pommery, now part of the rapidly growing Vranken champagne

© Champagne Pommery

empire, delights in its long association with the British market. It even designed its buildings in a French interpretation of the high Victorian neo-gothic British style that echoes the royal palaces and castles of England and Scotland.

Pommery's reputation was formed, like so many others, by the sterling efforts of a young widow. In 1858, just 22 years after the firm was founded and still only 39 years old, Madame Pommery took charge of the business. She had just lost a husband and had two young children, Louis and Louise – and to cap it all she knew virtually nothing about champagne. This disadvantage did not deter Mme. Pommery; she set out to listen, learn and taste. Under her control sales went from a modest 45,000 bottles in 1836 to 2 ½ million in 1890 – the year she died. In the 19th century Russia, with its taste for sweet wines, was champagne's premier market. Madame Pommery developed the drier Brut style that we all now enjoy especially for her British and American customers.

As you walk down the 116 steps that take you to a labyrinth of cellars, spare a thought for the 20 million bottles that rest in 'streets' named after the cities of the world where the name Pommery is synonymous with luxury. These cellars contain some of the most spectacular chalk carvings in the whole of champagne. It would be nice to think that the wine absorbs some of the grandeur of its setting throughout those long, dark months during which the all-important second fermentation and maturation complete their unhurried progress.

5, Pl. du Gal-Gouraud. Visit Monday to Friday during office hours, € appointments not always necessary. (Tel: 03 26 61 62 56 E-mail: info@pommery.fr)

Taittinger is a relatively new house even though it has a richly deserved reputation as one of the smartest of all Grande Marques. However, it was only in 1930 that Pierre Taittinger founded the firm. As a young soldier during the 1914-18 war he had been stationed south of Epernay at the impressive Château Marquetterie (marquetry). After the war he bought the château, named after the chequer-board vineyards of black Pinot and white Chardonnay vines originally planted by the monks, and started to make champagne.

Today Taittinger has extensive cellars in Reims. The most impressive of these are to be found beneath the ruins of the 13th century abbey of St. Niçaise. Stories are told of a secret tunnel that leads from the abbey to the basilica of St-Rémy.

There is a feminine, almost *haut-couture* elegance about Taittinger wines. They can be exquisitely perfumed, are always 'as smart as paint' and have the slim, elegantly long-legged appeal of an international 'cat walk' model. It was also, incidentally, the champagne chosen by Ian Fleming for his macho-hero James Bond.

Château Marquetterie and vineyard
© Champagne Taittinger

The company has long been a patron of the arts. In recent years it has been creating the Taittinger Collection, bottles of top cuvée vintage champagnes decorated with designs specially created for them by leading contemporary artists.

The popular visit includes some spectacular cellars as well as a visit to the disgorging room. 9, Pl. St-Nicaise, Monday to Friday, Appointments not always necessary. (Tel: 03 26 85 45 35)

Piper-Heidsieck, the champagne of the stars, was founded in 1780 by Florens-Louis Heidsieck. The son of a Lutheran pastor, he was a draper by trade and arrived in Reims in 1777 from his native Westphalia. On his death, in 1830, the house passed to his nephew Christian who went into partnership with his cousin, Henri Piper, and they adopted the name by which it is now known.

Ride by train through Piper-Heidsieck's cellars
© Champagne Piper-Heidsieck

Marilyn Monroe, who boasted that she only wore Chanel No. 5 in bed, was a great Piper fan and helped popularise the champagne in 'tinsel town'. Other Hollywood stars with a preference for Piper included Fred Astaire, Humphrey Bogart, Clark Gable and Ava Gardner as well as Laurel & Hardy. As a result the house, which is now owned by Rémy-Cointreau, exports some 60% of the five million bottles that it sells each year. The *Brut*, made from a blend of 85% Pinot Noir and Meunier and 15% Chardonnay, has fine bubbles and slightly citrus floral aromas.

Visitors travel around part of Piper-Heidsieck's 16km of cellar in an automatic vehicle that takes them on a magical journey to

discover the mysteries of the creation of champagne, brought to life in an explosion of light. Open every day from 1ˢᵗ March to 31ˢᵗ Dec., 9.30 to 11.45am and 2 to 5pm. €1, Blvd. Henry Vasnier. Appointment not usually necessary.
(Tel: 03 26 84 43 00 E-mail: visit@piper-heidsieck.com)

The story of **Veuve-Clicquot-Ponsardin**, to give this noble House its full name, is the stuff of which dreams are made. It was founded in 1772 by Philippe Clicquot who sent his first wines to Moscow in 1780 which, for the next 90 years, remained the House's main market. His son, François, had not long been married to Nicole-Barbe Ponsardin when he died in 1805 and, before her ailing father-in-law could sell the business, she took it over. She died in 1866, having revolutionised the champagne industry with her riddling stands and built up her company to become the household name that it is today.

The Widow
© *Champagne Veuve-Cliquot-Ponsardin*

King Edward VII loved his Veuve-Clicquot and would call for a 'spot of the Widow' when he felt like a glass, which was quite often. Hopefully, while he was still Prince of Wales, not within earshot of his mother, Queen Victoria. She would not have been amused!

Veuve-Clicquot, another member of the Moët-Hennessy group, has cavernous cellars containing around 40 million bottles of champagne, of which some six million are sold each year. The fascinating visit provides an insight into the complexities of 19ᵗʰ century business. € Monday to Saturday 1ˢᵗ April to 31ˢᵗ Oct. 10am to 6pm, Monday to Friday 1ˢᵗ Nov to 31ˢᵗ March. 10am to 6pm. 12, ru du Temple. (Tel: 03 26 89 53 90) website. www.veuve-clicquot.com

G.H. Mumm & Cie is another champagne house with a German pedigree. Peter-Arnold de Mumm, whose family made wine in the Rhine Valley, settled in Rheims in 1827. He was joined by his two grandsons, Jules and Georges-Hermann. Jules went off to form his own company and in 1852 the already prestigious house became known as G.H. Mumm. In 1904 Georges-Hermann took over his brother's business.

Then, in 1914, the business was seized by the government as the partners were still German nationals. After the First World War Mumm was taken over by a group of mill owners in the north led by a M. Dubarry. From 1945 to 1959 Mumm was run by the legendary René Lalou who set the highest standards and also opened a winery for sparkling wines in California in 1952. In 2000 the ownership of the company passed from the Canadian Seagram group to Allied-Domecq, a major British-owned drinks group.

© *Champagne Mumm*

As well as interesting cellar tours, both short and full length, for which no appointments are generally necessary, Mumm also offers a three-hour trip through part of their 218ha of vineyards, ending up at the windmill at Verzenay which has to be booked in advance. € Open throughout the year, closed 25th Dec. and 1st Jan., every day 1st March to 31st Oct. from 9 to 11am and 2 to 5pm: out of season weekdays and afternoons at weekends. 34, rue du Champ de Mars. (Tel: 03 26 49 59 70 E-mail: mumm@mumm.fr)

It would be wrong to leave the champagne cellars of Reims without mentioning three most important merchant houses –

Cellars at Charles Heidsieck
© *Champagne Charles Heidsieck*

Charles Heidsieck, **Lanson, Krug** and **Roederer** – who unfortunately do not have facilities for receiving casual visitors.

Charles Heidsieck, who founded his house in 1851, was undoubtedly the original Champagne Charlie. His self-publicising antics in London and New York helped him win big orders for his wines and even had a popular music hall song named after him. In 1985 the company was sold to Rémy-Martin and the cellar master, the late Daniel Thibault, began to set the champagne world alight with some spectacular wines that took the house to the top of the tree including his masterpiece, the 100% Chardonnay Blanc-des-Millénaires. His successor, Régis Camus, is already showing great skill but Daniel is a hard act to follow.

Krug, now controlled by Moët-Hennessy, was founded 1843 by Jean-Joseph Krug who came to France in 1835 and worked at Jacquesson in Dizy. All the base wine is made in small oak barrels. Unlike other producers who stress the importance of

The Krug Family
© *Champagne Krug*

their vintage champagne, Krug's top wine is its *Grande Cuvée*. This is a huge, profoundly rich and deep wine made from a Pinot Noir-led non-vintage blend with as much as 15-20% Pinot Meunier; the only world-class champagne to use such a significant proportion of this varietal. There is also an incredible *blanc de blancs* made from Chardonnay grapes grown in *Clos du Mesnil*, their enclosed vineyard in Les-Mesnil-sur-Oger on the *Côtes des Blancs*.

The house of **Louis Roederer** was actually founded by the Dubois family in 1776. Louis Roederer inherited the business in 1870 from his uncle and changed its name to his. Three years later he went to Russia and, determined to have his share of this lucrative business, he made friends with the stewards of all the noble houses, including Tsar Alexander II. Now the Tsar, who wanted his champagne to look different from all the others, was terrified of being assassinated. He thought that a small bomb could be placed in the 'punt' at the bottom of the bottle which is there to add strength to the bottle's weakest spot. Roederer returned to France and with much difficulty got the glassmakers to create clear, flat-bottomed bottles from lead crystal glass. Today Louis Roederer still make *Cristal* as well as seven other elegant styles that are more than just a cut above the average.

History Ancient & Modern

Porte Mars
© *OT Reims*

Reims is a city steeped in history. Although largely destroyed by German shelling in the First World War, you only have to look below the surface for traces of its glorious past. Conquering Gaul in 58BC, Julius Caesar defeated the local Celtic tribe, the Remi, who then swore allegiance to the Roman Eagle. As a reward Caesar made Reims the capital of his Imperial Belgian province and named it after the tribe.

The only above-ground remnant of the Roman occupation is the 3rd century three-arch *Porte Mars*, built by Agrippa to honour the Emperor Augustus Caesar who became his father-in-law. Several of its relief sculptures are still discernible, including the wolves who suckled Romulus and Remus. Among the finest Gallo-Roman remains in France is the 3rd century underground grain store, over two levels, on Pl. Forum. One of only five in the world, it can be visited without charge; there is also a small museum. (Tel: 03 26 50 13 74)

Roman grain store
© OT Reims

Christianity was brought to France in 496AD when Saint Remigus (St-Rémy) converted and crowned Clovis, king of the Franks. If you write the name Clovis in modern lettering, omitting the first letter, the 'v' becomes a 'u' and you have 'Louis,' the name chosen by 16 kings of France. St-Rémy was 96 when he died in 533, quite a remarkable age for those days. His remains are buried in the Romanesque basilica of St. Rémy that pre-dates the cathedral by almost 200 years. Alongside the church there is a museum, granted World Heritage status by UNESCO in 1991, whose priceless collection covers the history of Reims, regional archaeology as well as military history.

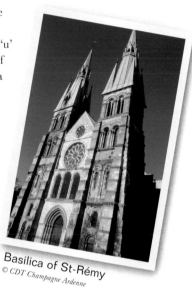

Basilica of St-Rémy
© CDT Champagne Ardenne

The cathedral of Notre-Dame de Reims, as we know it today, was started in 1211 and was intended to be the largest church in Christendom but just never got finished! For more than six centuries the Kings of France were crowned in the cathedral. It was here, in 1429, that Jeanne d'Arc (Joan of Arc) dragged the hapless Dauphin through crowds of English soldiers to his coronation as Charles VII. She then begged, without success, to be allowed to return to tend her sheep at Domrémy.

La Champagne has a long tradition as a centre for stained glass excellence. This reputation has been strengthened by the magnificent Marc Chagall blue windows, a glorious and fitting mid-20th century addition to a great Gothic gem; while on the north side there is a fascinating 1937 traditional stained glass window that tells the story of le champagne.

Reims Cathedral
© OT Reims

The **Vergeur Museum**, a merchant's house dating back to the 13th century, is in Pl. Forum. In 1523 the house was occupied by Nicolas Le Vergeur who gave his name to the building and added renaissance extensions. During the 17th century the house was owned by the Coquebert family and in the 19th century it became the home of the famous widow Clicquot-Ponsardin and her family. In 1910 the house was purchased by Huges Krafft (1853-1935) who in the previous year had formed the Society of Friends of Old Reims. He spent much of his considerable personal fortune restoring the house that had suffered much damage during the First World War. € Open every day except Mondays from 2 to 6pm and also from June to Aug. 10am to 12 noon. Closed 1st Jan., 1st May, 14th July and 25th Dec. 36 Pl. du Forum. (Tel: 03 26 47 20 75)

Vergeur Museum
© OT Reims

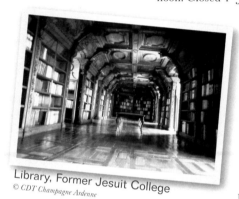

Library, Former Jesuit College
© CDT Champagne Ardenne

The former **Jesuit College**, on the way to the Basilica of St-Rémy, provides an insight into 17th century life. Visitors can see the rectory that contains a set of paintings by Jean Hélat portraying the life of St Francis-Xavier and Ignatius of Loyola, the founder of the Society of Jesus. The wood-panelled library, with its 18,000 books, is a masterpiece of French baroque architecture. € Visits every day, except Tuesday, Saturday and Sunday mornings and Bank Holidays, at 10, 11am, 2.15, 3.30 and 4.45pm. Allow 50 minutes for the tour. 1 Pl. Museux. (Tel: 03 26 85 51 50)

Attached to the former Jesuit College is the **Reims Planetarium**. € The programme is changed around every six months and, while the commentary is invariably in French, other languages are available by booking. 1 Pl. Museux. (Tel: 03 26 85 51 50)

Reims was a centre of both early aviation and motor sport. The French Grand Prix was held on a road circuit to the south of the city while a famous 12-hour race used to be run at Guex in *le petit montagne* to the west. This motor sport heritage is recalled by a collection of some 190 cars and motorbikes at the **Automobile**

Museum of Reims. € Open 1ˢᵗ April to 31ˢᵗ Oct. every day except Tuesdays, 10am to 12 noon and 2 to 6pm. Winter open weekends and holidays 10am to 12 noon and 2 to 5pm. 84, Av. Georges Clemenceau. (Tel: 03 26 82 83 94)

In 1945 General Eisenhower, supreme commander of the Allied Forces in Europe, set up his headquarters in what is today Reims' Technical College. It was here at 2.41am on the morning of Monday 7ᵗʰ May 1945 that the army, air force and navy of the Third Reich signed the unconditional surrender that brought to an end more than five years of carnage which had begun on 3ʳᵈ September 1939. The room where the declaration was signed has been classified as an historic monument and is now the Reims Museum of the Surrender. It is open to visitors every day, except Tuesday, 10am to 12 noon and 2 to 6pm, Closed 1ˢᵗ January, 1ˢᵗ May, 14ᵗʰ July, 1ˢᵗ & 11ᵗʰ Nov. and 25ᵗʰ Dec. 12, rue Franklin Roosevelt. (Tel: 03 26 47 84 19 E-mail: TourismReims@netvia.com)

Reims Museum of the Surrender
© *OT Reims*

Last, but by no means least of Reims' treasures, is the **Foujita Chapel**. Léonard Foujita, a Japanese painter of the Paris school, experienced a mystical experience while visiting the basilica of St-Rémy where he was later baptised with René Lalou of Mumm standing as his Godfather. Building began in 1965 to a design created, supervised and decorated by Foujita in the Romanesque style which, he considers, encourages a

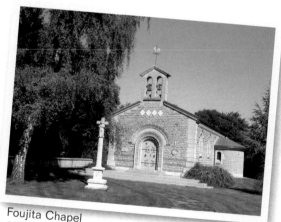

Foujita Chapel
© *OT Reims*

contemplative atmosphere while providing more space for his frescoes. Open from 2ⁿᵈ May to 31ˢᵗ Oct. from 2 to 6pm. Closed Wednesday and 14ᵗʰ July. (Tel: 03 26 47 28 44)

Shopping

Much of Reims had to be rebuilt after the First World War. The old medieval city had gone, so the architects devised new broad art-nouveau boulevards that provide both great views of the cathedral and wonderful spaces for shopping. These are also ideal sites for markets, most specially the famous Christmas *Village de Noël* Market from 28th November to Christmas Eve when you can buy everything to eat and drink as well as all your Christmas presents.

The Champenoise have a sweet tooth. Watch them on a Sunday, after Mass, buying delicious desserts to take home for their lunch from the many cake shops, or *pâtisseries*, that remain open all Sunday. Or join the ladies for a light lunch or afternoon tea at La **Bonbonnière**, 15 rue de l'Arbalète, close to the cathedral (open from 7.30am to 7.30pm closed Monday) or at fashionable **Waïda**, 5 Pl. Drouet-d'Erlon, open 7.30am to 7.30pm on Sunday, closed Monday, Tuesday to Saturday 7.30am to 1pm and 3.30 to 7.30pm.

Christmas Market
© OT Reims

© Champagne Ardenne

Chocoholics are well catered for by the **Deleans** family who have been *Chocolatier Maître Artisan* in Reims since 1874. The present generation, Vincent and Francesca, have their shop that dates back to the days of Marie-Antoinette at 20 rue Cérès, a five-minute stroll from the cathedral.

The delicate, pink-coloured *biscuits rosé de Reims* are another regional speciality and have been produced by **Fossier** since 1756. They can be used to surround desserts like Charlotte Russe, dunked into sweet drinks like Ratafia or Port or nibbled while tasting champagne. Fossier's shop is at 25, cours Langlet, a short step from the cathedral towards the station. They also have a shop at their bakery, 11 rue Péin (the other side of the station) which can be visited by appointment. (Tel: 03 26 40 67 67)

General de Gaulle once said that you cannot expect to rule a nation that produces 236 different cheeses. You'll find a great many of them at *le Cave au Fromage* in Pl. Forum but a word of warning; some may travel while others certainly won't! Also in Pl. Forum you'll find butchers shops specialising in the local ham, the famous *Jambon de Reims*.

Wine shops, many open on Sunday, are clustered around the cathedral. Others can be found along Pl. Drouet-d'Erlon, a wide pedestrian precinct that is the social centre of the city with friendly cafés and a wide choice of restaurants along its length. And, incidentally, a massive underground car park.

Excellent hypermarkets can be found at Tinquex (junction 22 off the Paris autoroute), Cormontreuil (junction 26 off the autouroute to Châlons en Champagne) and south on the N51 towards Epernay.

Restoring the inner man

Everything stops for lunch and, if you are around the cathedral at midday, then try and get a terrace table at the **Café du Palais**, 14 Pl. Myron-Herrick, close to the Place Royale. Popular with lawyers (from the nearby courts) and businessmen, this most traditional café has been run by the Vogt family since 1930 and Jean-Louis Vogt and his son will make you very welcome. Open Monday to Saturday 8am to 8.30pm.

Café du Palais
© OT Reims

You'll be spoilt for choice in the Pl. Drouet-d'Erlon. **L'Apostrophe** (No. 59) and **Brasserie Martin** (No. 7) are both good value while the **Taverne de Maitre Kanter** (No. 25) specialises in excellent seafood and Alsace choucroute. Or join the people of Reims at the massive **Grand Café** (No. 92).

In the market area is the **Brasserie du Boulingrin**, a bustling traditional restaurant full of atmosphere and champagne personalities, serving regional dishes and with great value champagnes. Closed Sunday. 48 rue de Mars (Tel: 03 26 40 03 92). On your way you will pass the **Jacquart**, at No. 6 rue de Mars. The entrance of this leading co-operative is shaped like a wine barrel, over the top of which are some magnificent mosaics showing the various champagne processes at the turn of the last century.

Allowing a couple of hours for lunch is normal. Dinner, on the other hand, is an even more leisurely meal, **Boulingrin** and

Maître Kanter are both as popular for dinner as they are for lunch. However, the different pace of life in the evening requires a special atmosphere that can be found at any of the following small selection of restaurants.

Table Anna is a comfortable and simple family restaurant with a distinctive style; the chef-patron is also the creator of designs that cover the walls and windows! You can eat and drink well for a modest price. 6 rue Gambetta, close to the National Conservatoire of Music & Dance. Closed Sunday night and Monday. (Tel: 03 26 89 12 12)

Place Drouet-d'Erlon
© OT Reims

The *Vigneron*, behind the cathedral, has a rustic setting complete with posters from the 1850s to the 1950s together with a collection of vineyard implements. The cooking is regional and space is limited, so booking is advised. Place P, Jarnot. Closed 5th to 19th Aug. Saturday lunch and Sunday. (Tel: 03 26 79 86 86)

The *Vigneraie's* classic cuisine and splendid wine list has made it extremely popular with the locals. A small restaurant, booking essential. 14 rue Thillois. Closed 4th to 24th Aug., Wednesday lunch, Sunday night and Monday. (Tel: 03 26 88 67 27)

The *Continental* is a stylish fin de siècle restaurant at the top of Pl. Drouet d'Erlon and one of the few places open on Sunday nights. Tables by the windows provide a wonderful view of the world passing by. 95 Pl. Drouet d'Erlon. Booking advised for Sunday nights. (Tel: 03 26 47 01 47)

The *Millénaire* (Millennium), Corinne and Laurent Laplaige's well-appointed elegant restaurant is in keeping with its location close to the Pl. Royale. Their cooking is very much up-to-date and full of flavours. 4-6 rue Bertin. Closed Saturday lunch and Sunday. (Tel: 03 26 08 26 62)

The Michelin-starred *Foch*, much frequented by leading champagne producers, offers beautifully presented classic dishes in an unhurried, intimate environment. 37 Blvd. Foch. Closed 27th July to 18th Aug. Saturday lunch, Sunday night and Monday. (Tel: 03 26 47 48 22)

Le Grand Cerf (the Big Stag) is a large elegant Michelin starred restaurant at Montchenot, 11km out of town on the N51 Epernay road. The cuisine is stylish and classic, the service is excellent and the setting splendid with a veranda that opens on to a garden. Booking recommended (Tel: 03 26 97 60 07)

Reims is fortunate in having two outstanding château-hotels with Michelin starred restaurants.

The multi-Michelin starred **Boyer Les Crayères** (the chalk caves) is an institution and, although M. Boyer may no longer be at the stove, the gastronomic experience continues uninterrupted by his well-trained team. The exclusive château accommodation is as elegantly luxurious as the restaurant. 64 Blvd. Vasnier. Booking essential. (Tel: 03 26 82 80 80
E-mail: crayeres@relaischateaux.com)

Palais de Tau et chevet
© OT Reims

L'Assiette Champenoise, just beyond the city at **Tinquex**, is another Reims institution. A beautiful château with a Michelin-starred restaurant, set in its own park with a large indoor swimming pool. The quite splendid restaurant is under the extremely able command of chef-patron M. Lallement, whose late father set culinary standards that he has managed to surpass. 40 Ave. Paul Vaillant-Couturier. Booking essential. (Tel: 03 26 84 64 64
E-mail: assiette.champenosie@wanadoo.fr)

Hotel rooms can often be in great demand, especially at weekends from May to October. Early booking is therefore strongly recommended.

Grand Hotel Templiers, once the elegant 19th century town house of M. Dubarry of champagne Mumm, is a now luxurious, elegantly appointed hotel with an indoor swimming pool. The 18 large rooms with bathrooms are superbly furnished, extremely quiet and exceptionally comfortable. No restaurant. 22 rue Templiers. (Tel: 03 26 88 55 08
E-mail: hotel.templiers@wanadoo.fr)

The city-centre **Hotel de la Paix** has recently completed extensive enlargement. This is where the British wine trade (and the author) stay when in Reims. No restaurant but linked to the *La Taverne de Maître Kanter*. Indoor swimming pool and Hot Room. Excellent relaxing bar. Well equipped comfortable bedrooms. Secure car parking. 9 rue Buirette. (Tel: 03 26 40 04 08
E-mail: reservation@hotel-lapaix.fr)

The **Porte Mars** is a well-insulated hotel on the Place Republique. No restaurant. A friendly wood-panelled hotel that prides itself on its gourmet breakfasts! 2 Pl. Republique. (Tel: 03 26 40 28 35)

The **Crystal** is a pleasant, modest hotel without a restaurant but with a garden where breakfast can be taken in summer. The rooms are small but well maintained. 86 Pl. Drouet-d'Erlon. (Tel: 03 26 88 44 44 E-mail: hotelcrystal@ wanadoo.fr)

Le Petit Montagne

Although close to Reims, *Le Petit Montagne* lies off the popular tourist route. Take the Paris autoroute, leave at the Tinquex turnoff (junction 22) and drive west towards Soissons. In a very short distance turn right towards Merfy. This is one of the villages that lie in an area called the St-Thierry vineyards after the nearby abbey of that name which, in the 9th century, was a cradle of vine growing.

You'll find **Chartogne-Taillet** on the *Grande-Rue* or main street. The family has been winegrowers in the village since the 17th century. They have 11ha of exemplary Pinot Noir and Chardonnay from which they produce beautifully balanced, refreshing and harmonious champagnes with sophisticated complexity. Excellent English. Visit by appointment only. (Tel: 03 26 03 10 17 E-mail: chartogne.taillet@wanadoo.fr)

The next village on the route is Trigny. Here you will find **R. Blin & Fils**, a highly respected winegrower whose Blanc de Noirs, with its nuts and citrus aromas, has won much acclaim. Visits by appointment, 11 rue de Point-du-Jour. (Tel: 03 26 03 10 97)

Continue west to Prouilly where winegrower **Jean-Marie Goulard** has an attractive chambre d'hôte. A pretty village with a church dating back to the 12th and 13th centuries, plenty of opportunities for walks with magnificent views. 12 Grande Rue. (Tel: 03 26 48 21 60)

Vineyards in summer
© *John Hodder/Collection C.I.V.C*

Students of modern history and the 1939-45 war will be interested in visiting the village of **Savigny-sur-Ardres** where General de Gaulle made his first radio appeal for the Resistance on 28ᵗʰ May 1940. There is a plaque on a house opposite the church that commemorates this event. From Prouilly follow the road south to Jonchery-sur-Vesle, cross over the river, go through the village, cross over the main road and take the D28 to Savigny-sur-Ardres. You can now return to Reims by the D27.

A Sunday of War & Peace
Fort de la Pompelle, Sillery & the nature park at Sept-Saulx

The First World War Fort at Pompelle
© *OT Reims*

Over the years Reims has been fiercely fought over but never with the ferocity of the First World War. **Fort de la Pompelle**, 5km south of the city on N44 – towards Châlons-en-Champagne – was built between 1880 and 1883, after the Franco-Prussian war of 1870, as part of a defensive system that was the forerunner of the Maginot Line. Stripped of its guns in 1913, it was occupied without a fight by the Germans on 4ᵗʰ September 1914. After the first Battle of the Marne the French infantry recaptured and held it for the next four years when it stood out against continuous onslaught, becoming a bastion in the defence of Reims. Today it is a museum that graphically shows what the Western Front looked like. Open from 1ˢᵗ April to 31ˢᵗ Oct. every day from 10am to 7pm, 1ˢᵗ Nov. to 31ˢᵗ March 10am to 5pm. Closed Tuesdays and from 24ᵗʰ Dec. to 6ᵗʰ Jan. (Tel: 03 26 49 11 85)

Leave the Fort and continue for around 1½km, turning right towards **Sillery** and the ***Relais de Sillery***. This pleasant waterside restaurant, with a pretty garden and tables on the terrace, serves classic dishes. Closed 16ᵗʰ Aug. to 5ᵗʰ Sept., Sunday and Tuesday nights and Monday. Book for Sunday Lunch. (Tel: 03 26 49 10 11)

Spend the afternoon in the **nature park** at nearby **Sept-Saulx**. Return to the N44 and continue for around 10km, turning left at **Les Petites Loges** bypass on to the D37 and Sept-Saulx and its glorious nature park. Children can play at Robinson Crusoe or try their hand at panning for gold, while the grown-ups can relax in the garden lulled to sleep by the bird song or the whole family can go boating. Or why not take a picnic and spend the whole day there? € Open April to Oct. daily from 10am to 6.30pm Closed Tuesdays April to June and Sept. to Oct. (Tel: 03 26 03 24 92 E-mail: parc.nature@wanadoo.fr)

Sunday in the Forest

Oak trees are an essential part of the French wine scene. When fully mature the trees are felled and, after drying out, they provide the staves from which barrels are made. The oak forest

Maison du Bûcheron
© CDT Champagne Ardenne

that once crowned the top of the Montagne de Reims has almost all gone but there are still parts that can be visited and these do give some idea of what it was once like.

Leave Reims on the N51 road to Epernay. After around 19km you will arrive at the cross roads with St-Imoges on your right and **Germaine**, a distance of around 4km, on your left. **La Maison du Bûcheron** (the lumberjack's house) is open each Sunday from Easter to 30ᵗʰ Sept. with a display of old woodworking tools and implements used by lumberjacks and more experienced craftsmen in past centuries.

For lunch, return to the main road and cross over towards **St-Imoges**. Almost immediately on your left is the ***Masion du Vigneron*** (the vineyard workers house) a rustic forest restaurant serving good food in a pleasing country environment. Closed Sunday night and Wednesday. Very popular on Sundays. (Tel: 03 26 52 88 00)

The Montagne

Leave Reims to the south on the N51 Epernay road
and, after a little over 10km, turn left on the *Routes des
Vins* towards Villlers-Allerand and **Rilly-la-Montagne**,
a *1ᵉʳ Cru* village on the north-facing slopes of the
Montagne and Champagne Vilmart & Cie.
Established in 1890, Vilmart is a family business with
11ha in 14 parcels of vineyard with 60% Chardonnay
and 40% Pinot Noir which are scrupulously
maintained without artificial fertilisers or chemical
sprays. They make their formidable champagnes

© *Huygens Daurigal/Collection C.I.V.C.*

using the most traditional of methods. All their base wines are
made and matured for at least ten months in either 50 hectolitre
oak *foudres* or casks or 220 litre *pièces* or barrels and have no
malolactic conversion. Following blending, the wines rest from an
absolute minimum of two years with up to four, five or more years
for the vintage.

Laurent Champs, whose mother was a Vilmart and the great-
granddaughter of the founder, makes the wines with an assurance
that belies his youth.

Like a number of growers he also makes a *Ratafia* but, while most
of them use what's left after the pressing, he insists on using the
same juice from which he makes his wine. The result is a
stunning apéritif that is a delight to sip on a warm summer's
evening. It is said to get its name from the Latin phrase with
which legal documents were once concluded – *Ut rata fiat* – a glass
often being enjoyed by lawyers and their clients once their
business was finished.

Visits Monday to Friday 9am to 12 noon and 2 to 5pm,
appointments not always necessary but preferred. Excellent
English spoken. 5, rue des Gravières. (Tel: 03 26 03 40 01)

For six generations the **Dalaunois** family have been winegrowers,
tending their vines and making champagne in Rilly-la-Montagne.
They produce around 60,000 bottles a year from their 8ha and
hold them for a long time on their corks before being disgorged.
Their winery seems to have changed little since it was first
opened in 1925, except for their intriguing revolving press. André
Dalaunois champagnes are masculine with a powerful structure
that is balanced by rich aromas and flavours. At first it might
appear that there is something hit or miss about this grower but
then they make their champagnes to please themselves and their
loyal customers, not to win awards; maybe they're not wrong!

The next village is **Chigny-les-Roses** which is as beautiful as it sounds and is full of great wine producers.

Winegrower **Jacky Dumangin**, on your right as you enter the village, only has 5.23ha but his champagnes have an elegant, intensely feminine air about them with acacia honey on the nose followed by light, eloquent flavours and a fine length. All Jacky Dumangin's work is based on respect: for his soil, his grapes, his wines and finally his customers. It's not surprising that one in three of his bottles are sold at the cellar door. The wines, which are bottled in May, will have rested on their corks for 18 months for the non-vintage Brut and 48 months for the vintage. 3, rue de Rilly. Visits from 9am to 6.30pm Monday to Saturday, Sunday by appointment. (Tel: 03 26 03 46 34)

Riddling
© *Frédéric Hadengue/Collection C.I.V.C*

Continue through the village till the road does a 'dog-leg' and here, on your right, you'll find **Cattier**, a family producer which has been cultivating vines since 1763 and selling champagne since 1918. It has the deepest cellars in Champagne dug out over three levels in the Gothic, Roman and Renaissance styles with 119 steps from top to bottom – although if you don't take the lift on the way back it seems much more!

Jean-Jacques Cattier and his winemaker son Alexandre have some 20ha of vineyards, the crown jewel of which is their 2.2ha of the Clos de Moulin, acquired in 1951. Wall-enclosed vineyards or clos are a great rarity in champagne and, although the ravages of war have seen both the walls and the windmill (*moulin*) disappear, the vineyard first planted in the reign of King Louis XV continues to provide some outstanding grapes. Each year some 15,000 bottles of Cattier's *Clos de Moulin* are produced. Both BA and Air France selected this most exclusive champagne for serving on Concorde. It is always assembled from wines from more than one vintage to create a most harmonious, almost honeyed, light elegance. 6-11 rue Dom Pérignon. Visits by appointment Monday to Friday and Saturday mornings. (Tel: 03 26 03 42 11 E-mail: champagne@cattier.com)

Tucked away in this village is the champagne house of **Georges Gardet** which was established in 1895 by the first Georges. He was succeeded in 1930 by his son Georges. The 1939-45 war was not kind to the Gardet family. A V2 rocket launch pad was built in their back garden and almost all of their precious stock of wine was looted. As soon as the war was over the second Georges and his sons set about resurrecting the business from scratch. Today the House is run by the founder's great-grandson, Jean-Philippe, a leading oenologist and former lecturer at the Champagne Academy in Avize. It is hoped that in time his son, Thomas, will be the fifth generation of the family running this great little house.

© *Champagne Canard-Duchêne*

The Gardet style is based on traditional values with the non-vintage Brut containing some very old reserve wines. Following a malolactic transformation the newly bottled blends rest on their corks for much longer than is usual. This achieves a full richness which combines beautifully refreshing acidity with the ripeness of excellent *1ᵉʳ Cru* fruit. Gardet champagne has that difficult-to-define English taste or *Goût Anglais* – a yeasty, almost maderised, flavour that fills the mouth with biscuity richness. 15, rue Georges Legros. Weekdays by appointment only. (Tel: 03 26 03 42 03 E-mail: info@champagne-gardet.com)

The road now leads to Ludes and two distinctly different producers, patrician Canard-Duchêne and rustic Ployez-Jacquemart.

The history of **Canard-Duchêne** goes back to 1835. Ignore, if you can, their hideous steel box on your left; the château lies off the first turning on the right. Like many houses Canard-Duchêne has had a number of owners and in 2003 Veuve-Clicquot sold it to Alain Thienot, although they kept the vineyards. The house is now run by Jean-Louis Malard. The cellars have an impressive display of works of art honouring the founders. The balanced and smooth champagnes contain wines from the *Côte-des-Bar*. The *Grande Cuvée Charles VII*, a blend of various vintages, is particularly fine. With a long connection with French cavalry regiments, Canard-Duchêne makes something of a speciality of opening bottles of champagne with a sabre! Well worth watching – but don't try this at home! € Visits every day except Sunday, April to Oct. 10am to 1pm and 2 to 5pm. 1 rue Edmond-Canard. (Tel: 03 26 61 11 60 E-mail: info@canard-duchene.fr)

Ployez-Jacquemart may be small but what this family house lacks in size it more than makes up for in quality. Laurence Ployez (excellent English) not only looks after their tiny vineyard and selects the pressed juice that they buy in from other farmers;

she also makes the wine. Her philosophy is to keep it simple. She uses no reserve wines at all and therefore technically makes vintage wines every year; however, only the top 20 to 25% of any producer's wines are allowed to be called vintage. Her style is expressive with a range of refreshing apéritif and more robust food-friendly champagnes. The family is proud of its long association with the RAF. Visits weekday 9 to 11am and 2 to 4.30pm, Saturday mornings by appointment. Mme. Claude Ployex. 9 rue Astoin. (Tel: 03 26 61 11 87)

Drive on east admiring the idiosyncratic modern sculpture on your right, just after the crossroads. This is not a TV aerial but a totem created by sculptor Bernard Pagès to represent a vine. You are soon in **Mailly-Champagne** which has one of the oldest and best co-operatives in Champagne. This is **Champagne Mailly Grand Cru** whose premises are on the left as you enter the village.

Reception at Champagne Mailly Grand Cru
© *Champagne Mailly Grand Cru*

Founded in 1929 its champagnes are made from grapes harvested from 70ha of Grands Crus vineyards – 75% Pinot Noir and 25% Chardonnay – within the village boundary owned by its 75 members. Individually they are only small farmers but together they form one of largest single sources of *Grands Cru* champagnes producing a range of some nine styles, 70% of which are entry level non-vintage Brut. The cellars hold more than 1,350,000 bottles, selling some 450,000 a year, half of them overseas.

The Mailly style is *Grands Crus* Pinot: fine floral aromas followed by rich fruit flavours, their *blanc de noirs* being particularly expressive. Commercial director Patig Morvezen, who comes from Brittany, is an accomplished Celtic student and will happily talk with visitors from Ireland, Scotland, Wales and even Cornwall in their own language. 28, rue de la Libération. € Visits without appointments weekdays 8am to 12 noon and 2 to 6pm, Saturday mornings 9am to 12 noon. (Tel: 03 26 49 41 10 E-mail: contact@champagne-mailly.com)

Mailly is also fortunate in having two excellent *chambres d'hôtes*, both with champagne connections. There is Mme. **Irène Chance's** spotless home just up the hill from the co-operative with a superb first floor en-suite bedroom that looks across her pretty little garden to the vineyards. 18 rue Carnot (Tel: 03 26 49 44 93). But if you prefer a working farm then stay with the

Malissart family who also have a garden and pets. Shared bathroom. **Annie-France Malissart**, 9 rue Thiers. (Tel: 03 26 49 4347 E-mail: afmalissart@infonie.fr)

© *Champagne Mumm*

The road now takes us along to **Verzenay**. Just before the village, on your left, is the famous **windmill** that now belongs to Mumm. Park your car and walk around the outside for a spectacular panoramic view. To your left is the city of Reims while to your front lie the vineyards and the autoroute with the newly built TGV (high speed train) line from Paris to Metz which is opening up the region to day visitors from Paris. Just the other side of the village, on the road to Verzy, you come across one of the strangest sights: a lighthouse set in the vineyards.

This is *le Phare* (lighthouse) *de Verzenay*. It was built in 1909 by the now extinct firm of Joseph Goulet to promote its champagnes. It is now a fascinating museum using audio-visual techniques to tell the story of champagne with cassettes in English to guide you on your way. Don't miss the old photographs of the wine farmers' revolt of 1911. Climb the tower for a bird's-eye view of the vineyards. (Tel: 03 26 07 87 87 E-mail: musee@lepharedeverzenay.com)

Michel Arnould & Fils have been growing vines in Verzenay for five generations. Patrick Arnould makes elegantly expressive wines exclusively from his grapes grown in the village, so there is nowhere better to experience the true taste of Verzenay. 28 rue de Mailly. Visits Monday to Saturday 9am to 12 noon and 2 to 4.30pm, Sunday by appointment.(Tel: 03 26 49 40 06 E-mail: info@champagne-michel-arnould.com)

You now continue to the village of **Verzy** and the highest point of the Montagne de Reims. **Louis de Sacy**, on your left, is a family merchant house

© *Museum Le Phare*

which has owned vines in the village since 1663. Today André and Alain Sacy make fine, vigorous and fruity champagnes from their 25ha spread across five *Grand Cru* villages, as well as buying in juice. 6 rue de Verzenay. Visits only by appointment. (Tel: 03 26 97 91 13 E-mail: contact@champagne-louis-de-sacy.fr)

Faux de Verzy
© CDT Champagne Ardenne

Au Chant des Galipes is a delightfully old-fashioned restaurant, in the centre of the town, serving market-fresh food that attracts diners from all over the region. 2, rue Chanzy. Closed 18th Aug. to 2nd Sept. and 22nd Dec. to 18th Jan., Sunday night, Tuesday night and Wednesday. (Tel: 03 26 97 91 40
E-mail: chantesgalippe@wanadoo.fr)

Return towards Reims and turn left (opposite Sacy) on to the D34; after a short distance on your left will be a sign to the **Faux de Verzy**, stunted beech trees that are one of mother nature's strangest creations. Park your car and follow the trail for around a kilometre or so and you will find the trees growing all over the forest, looking more like giant bonsai than anything else. St-Rémy and St-Basle from Lorraine once lived in this forest where there was an abbey which was destroyed during the Revolution. It is said that these tortured-looking trees are all that is left of the monks' garden. There is another tale that when Joan of Arc was escorting Charles VII to Reims for his coronation they came through the forest and, to help her find the way, she climbed up one of trees. Which is something you can't do today! It is a lovely walk in what is left of an ancient forest.

A whisky still in Champagne
© Distillerie Guillan

Carry on down the road and shortly before you reach the village of Louvois you'll be in Hameau (hamlet) de Vertuelle, which is where since 1997 Thierry Guillon has had his distillery producing **Whisky de la Montagne de Reims!** He learnt his trade in Germany distilling white fruit schnapps. He returned to his family home with some German stills and makes his whisky from a wash (brew) using local barley. Following distillation the spirit is aged in barrels of new French oak that give it powerful vanilla aromas. You can visit the distillery and sample his wares which are also available for sale together with other local gastronomic delights. Appointments preferred. Distillerie Guillons, Hameau de Vertuelle. (Tel: 03 26 51 87 50
E-mail: distilguillon@aol.com)

© Distillerie Guillan

Continue on to **Louvois** and turn right on to the D34 toward Bouzy; after a little way take the left turn to Bouzy through the vines. **Bouzy** – what a wonderful name for a *Grand Cru* champagne village – is an important source of outstanding Pinot Noir grown on the upper slopes.

Established in 1894, **Camille Savès** is a winegrower with 8ha all within the village boundary. Hervé Savès' advice on finding good champagnes is simple; 'Go to a good grower in a *Grand Cru* village who has well-aged stock'. He could be, and probably was, thinking of himself.

This is a producer who does not believe in allowing his wines to have a malo and, as a result, they do need longer on their corks for the fruit and acidity to come into balance. The *Brut Réserve* is a strapping expression of Bouzy Pinot Noir while the *rosé* is a robust pink, pungent with the aromas of ripe fruit. Camille Savès treat their still *Bouzy Rouge* very seriously indeed. It is only made from carefully selected grapes grown on the family's best sites and matured in oak barrels. 4, rue de Condé. Visits 8am to 12.30pm and 1.30 to 7pm Monday to Saturday. Little English spoken. (Tel: 03 26 57 00 33)

Driving into the **Pierre Paillard** courtyard you feel at once that this is a grower of some importance. There is an immediate sense of order and discipline. The house was founded in 1946 by Ulysse Paillard to grow grapes and ten years later launched its own champagnes. Benoît Paillard, the fourth generation of his family to work in champagne, farms his 10.65ha with the absolute minimum of artificial materials and keeps the yield down in order to add character and quality. He knows that 80% of his work is carried out in the vineyards and only 20% at the winery.

Benoît wants his wines to speak for themselves. He gives them the lowest *dosage* possible to achieve balance and the date of *dégorgement* is shown on back labels together with additional information. 2, rue XXème Siècle. Visits by appointment Monday to Saturday 9.30am to 12 noon and 2 to 5.30pm. (Tel: 03 26 57 08 04)

Jean-Paul **Brice** is a winemaker with a passion for the different flavours and textures created by the *terroirs* of the various villages. He formed his small merchant house in 1994. It produces champagnes made from grapes grown on the best sites in the villages of Aÿ, Verzenay, Bouzy – from his own 7ha – as well as a blanc de blancs from Cramant. A visit to this enthusiastic winemaker enables you to taste and compare the different villages and begin to understand the true importance of terroir. 22, rue Gambetta. Visits by appointment. (Tel: 03 26 49 77 44 E-mail: champagnebrice@wanadoo.fr)

Les Barbotines is Marie-Thérèse Bonnaire's impeccable chambre d'hôte in the centre of Bouzy. She combines great sparkling wine – her **Paul Clouet champagne** is now made in Cramant by her brother Jean-Louis Bonnaire – with the warmest hospitality, providing a haven where visitors can relax, leaving refreshed and set up for the day ahead after a most excellent breakfast. Stylish well-equipped en-suite bedrooms. Enclosed parking. 1 Pl. A. Tritant. (Tel: 03 26 57 07 31)

Our final stop on the Mountain, **Ambonnay**, is only a short step from Bouzy and our last winegrower is on the left, just as you enter the village.

This is **Marguet-Bonnerave** whose Brut Réserve was the very first champagne to be awarded a Certificate of Excellence by the Institute of Masters of Wine. It is a signal honour of which the family is understandably proud. The Bonnerave family began farming grapes in 1870 and in 1905 launched their own champagnes. Like all serious producers they know that to make fine wines you have to start with top quality grapes and they strictly follow eco-friendly sustainable methods without using any toxic chemicals. The family picks its grapes – 30% Chardonnay and 70% Pinot Noir – from the 13ha of vineyard that they own in three of the *Montagne's* top *Grand Cru* villages of Ambonnay, Bouzy and Mailly-Champagne.

Benoit Marguet (excellent English) is widely recognised as one of the up-and-coming young men in champagne. He is constantly developing and experimenting, searching for that most elusive of all things – the perfect champagne. So strong has been the support for the family's delicious rosés that they are slowly creating more of these beautiful pink wines – but only when the quality is absolutely right. The wines are matured in

© *Champagne Marguet-Bonnerare*

cellars that are still being dug out from under the family home. Legislation restricts these excavations to 'under property owned by the family or company'. The wine is kept considerably longer than that of many producers in order to create well-balanced champagnes with full and round flavours.

Benoit Marguet tastes in his cellar
© Champagne Marguet-Bonnerave

Such has been the demand for their wines that Benoit and his father Christian Marguet are now buying-in some grapes and juice that they are making into champagne under the Marguet Père et Fils label. The regular flow of cars with British number plates loading up in their yard is an indication of the following that the family has built up in the UK. 14, rue de Bouzy € Visits Monday to Friday during office hours, Saturdays by appointment. (Tel: 03 26 57 01 08 E-mail: benoit@champagne-bonnerave.com)

The *Auberge St-Vincent* in Ambonnay, named after the patron saint of vineyard workers, has a good kitchen that acquits itself well with a repertoire that might at first be considered to be a touch pretentious for a village inn. But then Mme. and M. Pelletier have always been ambitious. He is a most accomplished chef and she keeps her hotel, with its ten recently renovated rooms, in pristine condition. 1, rue St-Vincent. Closed 18th August to 1st September, Sunday night and Monday. (Tel: 03 26 57 81 48 E-mail: asv51150@aol.com)

This is the end of the Montagne de Reims tour; you can now either return to Reims by autoroute, drive to Tours sur Marne and then either to Châlons en Champagne or make your way to the Côte des Blancs.

The Côte des Blancs & Sézanne

Oh rapture! Oh pleasure! Oh joy!
The love of a girl for a boy
Remains so much stronger,
And lasts even longer
When pledged in Duval-Leroy.

EPERNAY

PIERRY

CHOUILLY

OIRY

CUIS

CRAMANT

N51

CÔTE DES BLANCS

CHÂLONS EN CHAMPAGNE

AVIZE

OGER

LE MESNIL SUR OGER

VILLENEUVE-RENNEVILLE

VERTUS

VOIPREUX

N33

ETRECHY

BERGÈRES LES VERTUS

COLIGNY

SÉZANNE

NOT TO SCALE

T he Côte des Blancs is a steep chalk escarpment that sweeps gently south for some 25km from Epernay. When the sun shines on the chalk it is easy to see the results of the earthquakes that ruptured the seabed some 30 million years ago. The Côte has a line of six *Grands Crus* villages beginning with Oiry, beside the river Marne, and running south from Chouilly, Cramant, Avize, Oger and finally Le Mesnil-sur-Oger, finishing on the plain at the 95% *Premier Cru* town of Vertus.

© *John Hodder/Collection C.I.V.C.*

This is Chardonnay country, with *blanc de blancs* being very much in evidence. The almost due east exposure catches all the morning sun which heats up the chalk and keeps the vines warm until late in the evening. Like the *Montagne*, the chalk is mainly belemites but not quite as deep, with mircaster on the lower slopes. The topsoil is a mixture of clay, carbon-rich lignite and sand with some flint in the south around Vertus.

The plain between Le Mesnil-sur-Oger and Vertus is prone to severe frosts in the early Spring and even up to May. Some growers have either installed smudge pots, which burn rags soaked in waste oil to heat up the air near the ground, or motorised propellers to blow the frosts away.

Although the smallest in overall surface area of the three northern vineyard regions, growers on the Côte do have some of the largest individual vineyard holdings.

The champagne college in Avize is the region's centre of educational and technical excellence. It is where most of the growers send their sons and, increasingly, their daughters to learn the secrets of the vineyard and the skills of the winery.

Sézanne, some 40km south of Vertus is a small unspoilt late 19th/early 20th century town at the centre of its own group of vineyards.

The Champagnes of the Côte des Blancs

Winegrowers dominate the Côte although, at its head and tail, there are two important co-operatives. The picturesque route along the D10 through the *Grand Cru* villages from Cramant to Le Mesnil-sur-Oger is well worth taking but travellers in a hurry may prefer the straighter D9. They will leave the main Epernay to Châlons-en-Champagne road at a roundabout and pass the huge St-Gobain plant whose tall red and white chimney is visible for miles around. This is where most of the champagne bottles are made, mainly from recycled glass. It is forbidden to re-use the bottles because any fault could cause it to explode due to the enormous pressure of the sparkling wine inside, so they are recycled.

We start our trip down the Côte at **Nicolas Feuillatte**, a massive modern co-operative on the D40 between **Pierry**, south of Epernay, and the *Grand Cru* village of Chouilly. In champagne terms

Bottling line
© Champagne Nicolas Feuillatte

this is a new organisation, only having been established in the mid-1980s when M. Feuillatte merged his 12ha Domaine St-Nicolas with *Centre Vinicole de la Champagne* who adopted his name for the brand. M. Feuillatte took on the role of roving ambassador, living in the USA and selling the wines all over the world.

A visit to this co-operative is like a trip to Planet Champagne. The whole operation is above ground in a huge air-conditioned building. Visitors travel between the different levels on gently inclined moving pavements allowing wheel chairs and prams to be manoeuvred with ease. The

Battery of gyropallets at Nicholas Feuillatte
© Champagne Nicolas Feuillatte

whole operation is in view, sometimes behind huge glass windows. Everything about Nicolas Feuillatte is on a massive scale. The juice comes in from 4,500 growers whose vineyards cover some 6% of the total area under vine and includes juice from ten Grands and 27 1er *Crus*. They have 206 stainless steel tanks holding a total of 160,000hl of wine. Their bottling line fills 20,000 bottles an hour while their 420 gyropallets are capable of riddling 210,000 bottles at a time. In 2004 they sold 7.1 million bottles world-wide, making them the fourth largest producer of champagne. The use of extremely sophisticated production equipment enables cellar-master Jean-Pierre Vincent to supervise production of these enormous quantities of champagne. The vintage and *cuvées* specials wines can be quite distinguished but the entry level nv Brut is light and frequently lacks charm. € Monday to Friday during office hours, weekends by appointment.
(Tel: 03 26 50 55 50)

Leaving Nicolas Feuillatte, you turn left towards Pierry and then left again at a roundabout towards Cuis.

With 26ha **Pierre Gimonnet & Fils** is one of the oldest and largest growers on the Côte and can trace its roots back to 1750. As befits its long history, the family's vines are equally ancient with over half being more than 40 years old and 70% upwards of 30 years old. The grapes harvested from their oldest vines, which are around 80 years old, seldom need chaptalisation; this is the permissible adding of sugar to the juice for the first fermentation. Low *dosage* for the Brut and vintage wines ensures that the Chardonnay's fresh and minerally flavours are not masked. 1, rue de la République. Visits Monday to Friday 8.30am to 12 noon and 2 to 6pm. Saturday morning by appointment. Very little English spoken. (Tel: 03 26 59 78 70)

And so on to the little hillside village of **Cramant**, made famous by Mumm when it produced a low-pressure sparkling wine, called a *Crémant*, which they simply styled as *Crémant de Cramant*. Although low-pressure wines are still made in Champagne, they may no longer be referred to as Crémant.

Diebolt-Vallois is a new house with old ideas making excellent champagnes from its 8.25ha, some with wood. The name is the combination of the husband and wife team who founded their business together in 1959 and still run it with the help of their children. The family's vineyards include plots in Cramant and Cuis, both planted with Chardonnay, and at Essoyes in the Aubea where they have 1.25ha of the two Pinots. Their entry level Brut, made from the traditional blend of equal parts of all three grape varieties, and the non-vintage *Blanc de Blancs* are both made in stainless steel. The vintage, Prestige and *Fleur de Passion* – launched in 1985 – are made or aged in oak. Visits by appointment. 84, rue Neuve. Excellent English. (Tel: 03 26 57 54 92)

Jean-Louis Bonnaire

There is something entertainingly infectious about **Jean-Louis Bonnaire** and his luxurious creamy champagnes with their fine focussed fruit. The business, founded by his maternal grandfather in 1932, now has 22ha in both the Côte and Marne Valley. A graduate of the Avize college, Jean-Louis cultivates his vineyards along eco-friendly lines with the use of organic fertilisers and treatment for endemic diseases kept to the minimum. He enjoys sharing his enthusiasm and knowledge of his wines with visitors eager to learn more about *le champagne*.

© *John Hodder/Collection C.I.V.C*

He also makes the wines from his sister's **Paul Clouet** vineyard in Bouzy. You might be fortunate enough to meet both Jean-Louis and Marie-Thérèse Bonnaire and experience both their wines at a tasting; that is if she's not back at her splendid *chambres d'hôte* in the centre of Bouzy. 129, rue d'Epernay. Visits Monday to Friday 9am to 12 noon and 2 to 5pm. (Tel: 03 26 57 50 85 E-mail: info@champagne.bonnaire.com)

Avize, with its champagne college, is only 4.5km further down the road. **Petit-Lebrun** is on your left as you enter the village. The Petit family planted their first vines in 1920 and five years later began selling champagne. Today they have 11ha spread over the five *crus* of Avize, Chouilly, Cramant, Oger and Oriy all planted with Chardonnay. Other than a rosé, for which they buy in the little Pinot Noir that they need, their champagnes are all *Blanc de Blancs*. The Pinot Noir comes from another grower in Cumières, in the Marne valley; growers are permitted to buy in, or exchange, up to 5% of their grapes. Holding their reserve wines for blending in oak barrels gives Petit-Lebrun's entry level non-vintage blanc de blancs a traditional and mature feel. Although the *dosage* of the vintage might appear a shade high it is a well-made wine with clarity of flavours and pleasing length. 10, rue de Lombardie. Visits by appointment. (Tel: 03 26 57 51 63)

Serious students of bio-dynamic and organic wines will be fascinated by **Domaine Jacques Selosse** but otherwise this is not a visit for anyone with only a passing interest in the subject. Anselme Selosse is an artist who creates his superbly stylish champagnes from 6.3ha of strictly organic vineyards, split over 42 separate parcels of land in Avize, Aÿ, Cramant and Oger. The secret of his success is preparing the ground so that its micro-organic population can thrive and support the vines to produce the finest, purest grapes possible. No petrochemicals are allowed anywhere near his vines. The soil is ploughed to get as much air into it as possible and help take down his special compost. This is made from equal parts of what's left over in the press, well rotted animal dung and vine prunings.

Anselme also follows the biodynamic approach to viticulture. This means that all his activities in the vineyard are governed by the position of the moon and stars. Although this does sound like all 'muck & magic', it does make senses: after all if the moon can exercise control over the oceans and their tides it can certainly control the flow of sap in a plant.

It takes over four hours to press a 4,000kg load in a Coquard press, the juice flowing directly to 200 litre oak barrels for fermentation and ageing. There is no period of settlement for the juice, nor is the fermentation assisted by adding sugar. The barrels contain juice from his separate

© John Hodder/Collection C.I.V.C.

parcels of land to which he adds the natural yeast collected from the same plots. His barrels are made for him by four different coopers and each one is made up from hand-riven staves from three different forests. This way he creates a harmony of flavours within his barrels which he describes as 'the lungs of his wines'.

He does not encourage a malolactic transformation. The barrels are stirred on their lees during fermentation but not after. His non-vintage wines are made in the barrel rather in the same way as Sherry, the barrels being topped up with younger wines so that the blending starts while the base wines are still maturing. Having made all the effort in the vineyard and placed his new made wine in, to quote Voltaire, 'the best of all possible worlds', he now leaves it well alone. Anselme Selosse will tell you that he has no right to interfere with his wines. Carbonic gas, naturally present in the barrels after the initial fermentation, keeps them free from oxidisation.

Everything that he does is done slowly and with logic. In June he starts to taste his wines and, if they talk to him and he understands what they are saying, he puts them into bottles. If not, then they are still too young and he leaves them until they are ready. The second fermentation in the bottle can last up to two to three months, compared with the same number of weeks in most other wineries. His non-vintage wines spend at least 30 months maturing before being disgorged. The length of time that the vintage stays in his cellars depends upon how long it needs. The date of disgorging always goes on to the back label.

When young, and recently disgorged, the levels of oak and autolysis – the flavours from dead yeast broken down by its own enzymes – can be enormous but left to age in the bottle his champagnes become extraordinarily harmonious. Anselme

Selosse is a man who breaks all the rules to create great champagnes. He doesn't talk about the taste of his wines in vernacular wine-speak. This is because he doesn't taste for aromas or flavour, rather he tastes in the same way that he listens to music – for harmonies, not single notes. 22, rue Ernest Vallé. Visits strictly by appointment and please only by those with a serious interest in bio-dynamic and organic wines. (Tel: 03 26 57 53 56)

Manuel de Sousa was a Portuguese soldier who stayed behind after the 1914-18 war, ending up in Avize and marrying a winegrower's daughter. His grandson, **Erick de Sousa**, has 6ha in Avize, Cramant, Oger and Epernay. He is another bio-dynamic wine-maker who partly makes his wines in oak barrels and uses generally low *dosage*. The result is a pure and complex range of *Blanc de Blancs* champagnes that can have a magnificent mineral character with terrific complexity and length of flavour. M. de Sousa makes wines that are a perfect match for *Grande Cuisine*

© *Champagne Nicolas Feuillatte*

which is perhaps why they are frequently found on the wine lists of equally great restaurants. 12, Place Léon-Bourgeois. Visits by appointment. Little English. (Tel: 03 26 57 53 29)

Opposite the champagne college at 14 Route d'Oger you'll find Le Vieux Cèdre, the charming home of **Pierson Whitaker**, a new and small family champagne business run by Didier Pierson and his charming English partner Imogen Whitaker. Didier is only just starting out on his champagne adventure while Imogen runs their delightful *chambre d'hôte* where English is spoken by herself and their children. Didier does well to keep up.

The Clos de Mensil
© *Champagne Krug*

Quiet en-suite rooms, one with a bath in the middle! Generous breakfasts. Table d'hôte dinner can be booked in advance. No pets but you can share theirs. No smoking. (Tel: 03 26 57 77 04)

A short 1.5km and you are in **Oger**, a very pretty village whose excellent vineyards are invariably owned by winegrowers in other villages. Drive on another 2km and you are in **Le Mesnil sur Oger** which could claim to be the most important village along the Côte. As well as being home to Krug's tiny but celebrated Clos-de-Mesnil, it is also where you'll find **Salon**. This most singular house produces just one champagne, a 100% *Grand Cru* vintage *blanc de blancs* made exclusively from grapes harvested from the best sites in Le-Mesnil; and then only in the best years.

It was created by Eugène-Aimé Salon, a native of champagne who had gone to Paris at the turn of the last century and became a successful, fashionable furrier. He moved freely among the city's high society and very much enjoyed partying, so much so that he wanted to serve his own champagne at his own parties. In 1911 he got together with his brother-in-law, who was then cellar-master at Veuve Clicquot, and between them they devised a most radical approach to making champagne which, in those days, was always 75% Pinot. They decided to make their wines only from Chardonnay grapes harvested from the top plots in the then newly-elevated *Grand Cru* village of Le Mesnil; and then only in outstanding vintages.

Their plans were interrupted by the 1914-18 war so it wasn't until 1921 that they produced their first champagne and then again in 1923 and 1925. In 1928 Maxim's, the restaurant loved by the Paris 'smart set', bought it as their house champagne and demand took off. However, production remained extremely limited, adding to its reputation as the most elusive and exclusive of all champagnes. Since 1989 Salon has been owned by Laurent-Perrier who continue to retain the character and style laid down by Eugène-Aimé. The house never receives visitors.

Champagne Launois Pére et Fils
© Benoit Marguet

Among the most fascinating visits in the whole of champagne is that to **Launois Père & Fils**, who are one of the largest and most important growers on the Côtes des Blanc. Bernard Launois is an entrepreneur who not only sells his juice to such leading merchant houses as Lanson and Ruinart but also makes his own champagnes. Yet he still finds time to devote to his passion of collecting champagne and vineyard memorabilia. This collection is housed in a museum which forms the focal point for his regular visitors who come by coach from all over France, Belgium and Germany. They not only visit the winery and the fascinating museum but also have lunch in a

Ready for lunch in the cellars
© Champagne Launois Pére et Fils

splendid dining room before going away with their coaches groaning under the weight of the champagne they are invariably carrying.

The quality of these champagnes has been enhanced by his new press house, with the latest inclined plate presses, which he has built in the vineyards. Bernard makes expressive *blanc de blancs* champagnes from his 22ha of Chardonnay vineyards in the Côtes des Blancs and a further twelve in Sézanne. He produces a whole family of eloquent champagnes by blending wines from small parcels of his extensive holdings. The lean and long *Cuvée Réserve*, which has rested on its lees for a full three years, makes an excellent apéritif while the fuller and rounder *Veuve Clémence*, named after the founder's widow, is perhaps more to the 'English' style. The Launois family – Bernard, his charming wife Danni and two daughters – are exceptional hosts. 2, Ave. Eugène-Guillaume. Excellent English spoken when his son-in-law, Benoit Marguet (from Marguet-Bonnerave in Ambonnay) is there! Visits by appointment any day including Sunday mornings. (Tel: 03 26 57 50 15)

Harvesting Chardonnay
© Champagne Nicolas Feuillatte

Pierre Péters, founded in 1940, is run today by his son François whose brother Jacques is the *chef de cave* or cellar master at Veuve Clicquot. François is a most innovative wine maker producing some 135,000 bottles of champagne a year from his 17.5ha of vineyard in Le Mesnil, Oger, Avize, Cramant and Vertus as well as Sézanne.

His vines, with an average of around 25 years of age, are 95% Chardonnay with only 3% Pinot Noir and 2% Pinot Meunier. Following pressing and settling the base wine is made in stainless steel vats which enhance their light style, allowing Chardonnay's delicate tones to be fully expressed. In good vintage years the base wine can have all the richness and complexity of a top Côte de Beaune. Among the most successful of all François's wines is his beguiling Perle-du-Mesnil, a crémant style *blanc de blancs*, with just 3½ atmospheres behind the cork. 25, rue des Lombards. Visits by appointment. Monday to Friday 8am to 12 noon and 1.30 to 6pm. Little English. (Tel: 03 26 57 50 32 E-mail: champagne-peters@wanadoo.fr)

Mesnil is also the name a restaurant situated in an old house at the back of the town where you will find classic French dishes accompanied by a most discriminating wine list. 2, rue Pasteur.

Closed 17ᵗʰ Aug. To 7ᵗʰ Sept, Monday and Tuesday nights and Wednesday. Bookings essential for Sundays. (Tel: 03 26 57 95 57 E-mail: mesnil@chez.com)

As you drive the 5.5 km to **Vertus** look to your left, on to the plain, and see the large propellers set in the vineyards. These are fired-up as soon as there is a threat of frost to keep it away from the vines.

Vertus, the final town of *the Côtes des Blancs*, has some 534ha of *Premier Cru* vineyards with 138 winegrowers, five merchant houses and five co-operatives. It is a busy little town that provides a quiet base for a couple of nights visiting the region.

The family-owned House of **Duval-Leroy** was formed in 1859 when Jules Duval merged his firm with that of Edouard Leroy. Today its success, like that of so many other champagne houses in the past, lies in the hands of a young but tough and capable widow, Carol Duval. Her husband, Jean-Charles, died suddenly in 1991 and left her in charge of 142 hectares of vineyards, some 120 employees and more than 14 million bottles maturing in the family's cellars at Vertus and Châlons-en-Champagne.

Born in Belgium, Carol Duval, like all the champagne widows before her, was quite unprepared for the task. Yet under her chairmanship the house, with its reputation for good value, has moved into the top ten with the capability of producing some 6¹/₂ million bottles a year. It is fascinating to consider that Duval-Leroy is already better known on more markets than Clicquot-Ponsardin was at the time that the most famous champagne widow of all, La Veuve Clicquot, took over.

Madame Duval is fortunate to have at her right-hand side a most distinguished cellar master, Hervé Jestin. He has used the family's substantial investment to create a superbly equipped press house and a state-of-the-art winery. Duval-Leroy produces a full range of champagnes under the *Fleur de Champagne* brand. The base wines are given a malolactic and the rosé is made by macerating rather than blending in red wine before the second fermentation in bottle. The non-vintage wines are aged for two to three years on their corks while the vintages rest around seven years before they are disgorged. It is a house whose champagnes are highly acclaimed for their elegance, purity of fruit and consistency. 69, Ave. de Bammental (turn left almost as soon as you

© CIVC

enter the town, over the level crossing and it's on your left) Visits by appointment Monday to Friday 8am to 12 noon and 2 to 6pm. (Tel: 03 26 52 10 75 E-mail: champagne@duval-leroy.com)

In the centre of the town is Paul Goerg, a progressive co-operative formed in 1950 as *La Goutte d'Or* (the golden drop) with just 19 wine-farmers. They took their brand name from Paul Goerg, a 19th century regional councillor and former mayor of Vertus. Today *La Goutte d'Or* has 110 producers farming some 120ha of *Premier Cru* vines on the Côtes des Blancs that are made into a full range of Chardonnay-rich champagnes with well-focussed flavours. *Brut Tradition* with its lemony, well-structured character, accounts for 70% of the production and is a blend of 60% Chardonnay and 40% Pinot Noir with around 50% reserve wines. 30 rue Général Leclerc. Visits Monday to Friday 8am to 12 noon and 2 to 6pm, and 9am to 12 noon Saturday. Open on Sundays from Easter to Harvest 11am to 5pm. (Tel: 03 26 52 15 31 E-mail: champagne-goerg@wanadoo.fr)

Elizabeth **Larmandier-Bernier**, and her son Pierre Larmandier, have 11ha of mainly Chardonnay vineyards in some 37 parcels in Vertus, Cramant, Avize and Choully. The Lamandier family has been involved with farming grapes since well before 1789, the year of the French Revolution, and entered the champagne business in 1900.

© Collection C.I.V.C

Pierre (excellent English) is a most accomplished young winemaker who sells over half of his production outside France which, for a winegrower, is quite remarkable. He is the first to admit that he does nothing different, he just lets the *terroir* talk through his wines. Yet the obvious care and attention that he lavishes on his vineyards and during winemaking results in deliciously creamy and crisp champagnes. Balance, finesse and freshness are the hallmarks of his range of seven champagnes. There is also a *Coteaux Champenois* made from their Pinot Noir vines in Vertus which is also used to make his fruity rosé. His most remarkable wine is a *Blanc de Blancs* made without *dosage* exclusively from the best sites of their Vertus vineyards. Harmonious and long, it has aromas and flavours of honey, flowers and Earl Grey tea (bergamot). 43, rue du 28-Aout. Visits only by appointment. (Tel: 03 26 52 13 24)

The chalet-styled ***Hostellerie de la Reine Blanche*** (white queen) with its restaurant ***Le Thibault IV*** is a popular weekend stopover.

This hotel has an indoor heated swimming pool and fitness centre and offers attractively-priced inclusive two-day breaks. Rooms in the annexe are bigger and better equipped. 8, Ave. Louis Lenoir. (Tel: 03 26 52 20 76)

Just south of the town at **Bergères-les-Vertus** is the **Hostellerie du *Mont-Aimé*** which Annie and Jean Sciancalepore have built up over the years from the village bar. They have created a comfortable, reasonably priced hotel with well-equipped rooms (some a fair way from the hotel's reception), a restful garden, car parking, outdoor swimming pool and an excellent restaurant. Closed Sunday nights. The hotel takes its name from the nearby Mont-Aimé where Wellington and the allied generals met after the battle of Waterloo to share the spoils of war. (Tel: 03 26 52 21 31 E-mail: mont.aime@wanadoo.fr)

If you have ever wanted to stay in a romantic moated 17th Century château then *Le Château d'Etoges* could be exactly what you have been looking for. Etoges lies 17km west of Bergères-les-Vertus on the D 933 Montmiral road. Set in its own park the château is an historic monument with 20 bedrooms and a gastronomic restaurant. (Tel: 03 26 59 30 08 E-mail: etoges@wanadoo.fr)

On to Sézanne

© CDT Champagne Ardenne

Leave on the D5, direction **Fère-Champenoise** 14km away, with the Mont-Aimé on your right. At Fère-Champenoise turn right on to the N4 Paris road for 19km. **Sézanne** is a small, mainly medieval town unafflicted by the worst excesses of 20th century architecture and largely free from the horrors of 'modern' shop fronts. It is France as she was at the turn of the 20th century; cobbled streets, gently shaded walks and proud squares. The town is dominated by the monumental square tower of the church of St-Denis that dates back to the 16th century. The tourist office beside the church will provide you with a whole host of information.

The original fortified walls have become a series of shady walks known as

The Church at Sézanne
© OT Sézanne

© OT Sézanne

Les Mails, each of which has an historic name. There is *Des Cordeliers* named after the monks who settled in 1293 alongside the ramparts; *Des Religieuses* refers to where the Abbaye du Bricot once stood; while *De Marseille, du Mont-Blanc* and *de Provence* recall the national guardsmen sent to the town in July 1790 to celebrate the Federation following the revolution and quartered on the *mails*. Stroll along the town's picturesque old lanes like the rue Cognfort, rue de Teinturiers (dyers), ruelle (little street) aux Chats (cats), La Queue-du-Renard (the fox's tail) and la Cour Bichot.

Water was the sole source of medieval power. However, because Sézanne has no river, in the 12th century they diverted part of the river Morin to create *la Rivière d'Auges* which coursed through the town driving water mills to power weavers looms. One of these water mills, *le moulin de Broyes*, can still be seen.

The town's great moment of glory was the 31st August 1725, when Maria Lesczynski – daughter of King Stanislaus of Poland – stayed at the house of the Duc d'Orleans on her way to marry Louis XV. Not far from this house there is a giant sundial painted on the wall that dates back to 1783. Just around the corner is the old market hall, *La Halle*, built in 1892 and refurbished in 1988/89.

The town is fortunate in having two comfortable inns in the rue Notre-Dame that provide simple accommodation and excellent meals in their restaurants. ***Le Relais Champenois et du Lion d'Or*** is a family business where Madame Fourmi runs the front of house while her husband prepares wonderful meals in the kitchen. ***La Croix d'Or***, a little further up the road, also has a range of varied rooms and a restaurant that also offers very good meals at reasonable prices.

Le Relais Champenois et du Lion d'Or, 157 rue Notre-Dame. Closed 20th Dec. to 5th Jan and Sunday night. (Tel: 03 26 81 35 32 E-mail: relasichamp@infonie.fr)

La Croix d'Or. 53 rue Notre-Dame. Closed 15th Aug., 18th Oct., 22nd Jan. to 1st Feb., Sunday night and Tuesday. (Tel: 03 26 80 61 10)

Vineyards nestle around the north of the town in a sort of amphitheatre. **Congy**, one of the main champagne villages in the region, is some 20km north on the main road to Epernay, the

D951. Follow this road for around 16km and then past **Baye** take the first turning right.

In the centre of Congy you'll find **Breton Fils**, family winegrowers since 1952, who have 17ha planted with all three champagne grapes. Their cellar isn't very deep but it must have the steepest stone steps with the lowest head height of any you will ever come across! But don't worry, they bring you up another way to their friendly tasting room where you can sample their crisp, refreshing champagnes made with the ripe fruit for which the Sézanne's vineyards are famed. You are sure of warm welcome from Nathalie and Johann Breton; they know that their village is not on the regular tourist routes and they look forward to tasting their wines with visitors from outside France. 12, rue Courte-Pilate. Appointments preferred. (Tel: 03 26 59 3103)

Collecting Capsules

Capsules are the printed metal caps placed over the cork and under the wire muzzle. They have become collectors' items with houses producing different designs of capsule for their various styles of champagne. Girls in the region are even studding them on to their belts or making bracelets from them. If you are a regular champagne drinker, or plan to become a frequent visitor to the region, then why not start your own collection mounted on cork-boards and hung in the kitchen?

© *Cephas/Joris Luyten*

The Aube

Pinot from Aube's vinous farms,
Blended with wines from the Marne,
Adds freshness and fruit
To the most humble Brut,
For champagnes of incredible charm.

Troyes (pronounced 'Twar' with a short 'a') is 118km, or 1½ hours, by *Autoroutes* A4 and A26 from Reims. The old capital of the Counts of Champagne, this medieval city stands at the threshold of the vineyards of the Côte des Bar at Bar sur Aube and Bar sur Seine, as well as the singular region of Montgueux. Called by some the Montrachet of champagne, Montgueux is an outcrop of chalk 10km west of Troyes that rises 270m above vast cereal plains.

It has 180ha of south-facing vineyards, 85% of which are superb quality, early ripening Chardonnay. These grapes attract the cellar-masters from the large merchant houses of Epernay and Reims who want them for their top *cuvées*. The law of supply and demand drives up the price far beyond its low classification.

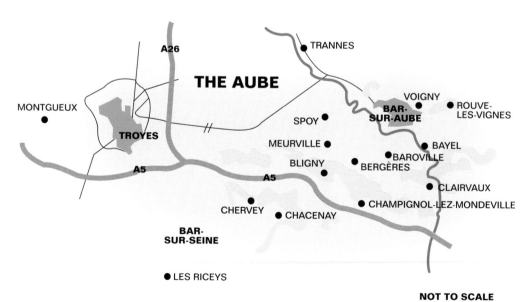

Within easy reach of Troyes is a 70,000ha national park with three giant lakes, as well as Nigloland, France's third most popular attraction after Disney and Asterix. Other places of special interest are Colombey-les-Deux-Eglises, where President de Gaulle had his family home, and crystal glass works at Bayel founded by a French queen to provide the stemware for her palaces. And then there is Essoyes where the artist Renoir lived and worked and where you can visit his studio.

The Côte des Bar is champagne's secret vineyard. It is a land steeped in history where agriculture and viticulture sit side-by-side in perfect harmony. In autumn tall sunflowers bend their heads in deference to the corn which stands not quite as high as an elephant's eye while cattle gently graze along the lush banks of the rivers Aube and Seine. And on the rolling hills, carefully tended lines of ripening Pinot Noir vines wait patiently for pickers to come and cut their plump, black pendulous bunches.

© John Hodder/Collection C.I.V.C

Spread over some 7,000ha the Côte des Bar vines account for a quarter of the total champagne vineyards. They are planted with 85% Pinot Noir, around 12% Chardonnay and a rapidly diminishing 3% of Pinot Meunier. Much of the region's pressed juice and wines are shipped up to the big merchant houses in the north to provide the backbone for their non-vintage Brut and to meet the steadily growing demand for pink champagne.

With its kimmeridgian clay sub-soil it is a land far removed from the chalk slopes of the *Côte des Blancs* or the *Montagne de Reims*. Unlike Epernay and Reims, here there are not many grand mansions reflecting Napoleonic splendour but plenty of winegrowers creating good, honest champagnes rich with the juice of the Pinot Noir.

The Côte des Bar is a land of pretty villages with half-timbered houses and ancient churches. It is a region where visitors are welcome but growers concentrate far more on making their wines than providing cellar tours. This is not because they are inhospitable-indeed, just the reverse-but because they are off the well-beaten tourist track and don't see that many visitors.

In spite of its medieval history, the Aube is thoroughly up-to-date when it comes to helping visitors navigate around the region. For ten euros a day and a refundable deposit of 200 euros (all on credit card) you can hire Hoppy, a GPS (global positioning system) that fits on to the dashboard of your car and guides you on your way with an English commentary. You can pick a system up from the *Comité Départmental de Tourisme de l'Aube en Champagne*, 34 Quai Dampierre, Troyes in the old city. Best telephone first to reserve a set. (Tel: 03 25 42 50 00)

Troyes en Champagne

The city was founded around 20BC as a staging point on the Imperial Way built by Agrippa, the Roman road that linked Milan to Boulogne. In 451AD Attilla the Hun was halted in his tracks at

TROYES

Boucherat (R.)	**CY** 4	Huez (R. Claude)	**BYZ** 27
Champeaux (R.)	**BZ** 12	Israël	
Charbonnet (R.)	**BZ** 13	(Pl. Alexandre)	**BZ** 28
Clemenceau (R. G.)	**BCY** 15	Jaillant-Deschaînets	
Comtes-de-Champagne		(R.)	**BZ** 29
(Q. des)	**CY** 16	Jean-Jaurès (Pl.)	**BZ** 31
Dampierre (Quai)	**BCY** 17	Joffre (Av. Mar.)	**BZ** 33
Delestraint		Langevin (Pl. du Prof.)	**BZ** 35
(Bd Gén.-Ch.)	**BZ** 18	Marché aux Noix	
Driant (R. Col.)	**BZ** 20	(R. du)	**BZ** 36
Girardon (R.)	**CY** 22	Michelet (R.)	**CY** 39
Hennequin (R.)	**CY** 23	Molé (R.)	**BZ** 44
		Monnaie (R. de la)	**BZ** 45
		Paillot-de-Montabert	
		(R.)	**BZ** 47

Palais-de-Justice (R.)	**BZ** 48
Préfecture	
(Pl. de la)	**CZ** 49
République	
(R. de la)	**BZ** 51
St-Pierre (Pl.)	**CY** 52
St-Rémy (Pl.)	**BY** 53
Synagogue (R. de la)	**BZ** 54
Tour-Boileau	
(R. de la)	**BZ** 59
Trinité (R. de la)	**BZ** 60
Turenne (R. de)	**BZ** 61
Voltaire (R.)	**BZ** 64
Zola (R. Émile)	**BCZ**
1er-R.A.M. (Bd du)	**BZ** 69

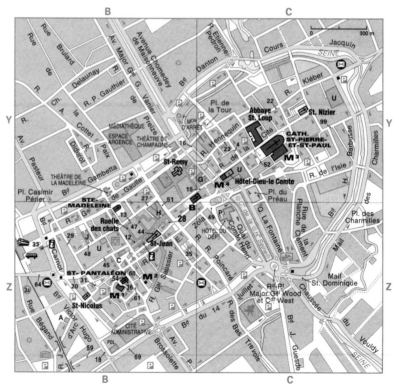

the city's gates by Bishop St-Loup which was as far west as this notorious invader got.

The ancient capital of Champagne, laid out like a champagne cork, can justifiably claim to have invented shopping! Thibaud the Great, Count of Blois and Champagne (1088-1152) brought craftsmen and tradesmen from all over the known world to the city and so established the first Champagne fair, or market, where goods could be bought and sold. It is a custom that still continues to this day; in the 1960s Troyes had the world's first factory outlet shops that sold off the surplus production from its numerous hosiery factories.

Culture

The city centre lies east to west, with the river Seine providing the eastern limits, and attractive tree-lined boulevards with plenty of car parking space. A canal with wide quays divides the centre into two. To the east, in the mushroom shaped head of the cork, is the cathedral of St-Pierre and the university. The west, in the straighter body of the cork, is more commercial with the markets and a number of pedestrianised streets with shops of all shapes and sizes.

The cathedral of St-Pierre, built between the 13th and 16th centuries, has some exquisite stained glass. Unfortunately the steeple was never finished because the money to build it ran out!

16th Century Chancel Screen
© Ph Praliaud/CDT Aube

The ancient church of St-Jean-au-Marché near the tourist office in rue du Mignard is of special interest to the English because it was where King Henry V married Catherine de Valois, daughter of King Charles VI of France, on 2nd June 1420. The previous month Henry and Charles had signed the Treaty of Troyes which, following the battle of Agincourt, made Henry heir to the French crown. Nine years later Joan of Arc led Charles VII to Reims and freed it from the English. The church is currently undergoing much needed extensive restoration.

The 13th century **Basilica of St-Urbain** is a pure gothic jewel. It was founded by Pope Urban IV, who was born in Troyes in 1185 as Jacques Pantaléon, on the site of his father's cobbler's shop. In 1645 the church became the headquarters for a brotherhood of painters, glassmakers and embroideries that flourished in the city.

At the time that Pope Urban IV was raising his Crusade Hughes de Payen, who came from just beyond Troyes, was forming a band of soldiers dedicated to defending the monks who were going on the Crusade. They became the Knights Templar and over time a most powerful order which, during one period, owned much of the city of Troyes and lands around.

Troyes Cathedral
© D. Le Neve/Ville de Troyes

Ste-Madeleine is the oldest church in Troyes. A most extraordinarily delicate lace-like chancel screen, carved in stone by Jean Guailde early in the 16th century, divides the choir from the main body of the church in the rue de la Madeleine. They say that its creator is buried beneath his masterpiece and that his epitaph reads, '*May he await the blessed Resurrection without being squashed*'.

As you walk around the city, admire the special Champagne chessboard use of brick and limestone on the lower walls with the half-timbered and plaster structures above that lean out over the pavements. In medieval times taxes were levied on the surface of the ground floor only, so the upper floors were built with overhangs to provide more tax-free space. It also allowed the slop pails to be emptied from the upper floors directly into the drains that then ran through the middle of the streets. Not very hygienic!

Eating and drinking in Troyes
© Ph Praliaud/CDT Aube

Extensive careful restoration, still being undertaken in the old city, is a fitting tribute to Troyes' tradition as a great centre for arts and crafts. Contemporary craftsmen in wood, metal and stone are intrigued by the museum of what is described as 'Tools and Working Class Thought' at the 16th century **Hôtel de Mauroy**, rue de la Trinité (Tel: 03 25 73 28 26). Perhaps it's not surprising to discover that since 1989 Troyes has been home to Europe's first university for craftsmen.

Since the early days of the fairs Troyes has been a centre of fabric and fashion. At first this was the simple knitting of stockings and making of bonnets and other garments. Then in the 18th century the invention of the loom enabled the city to become an important centre for the manufacture of clothing of all types. By the turn of the 19th century Troyes had 420 mills and 260 stocking manufacturers. All of these are recalled in the **Hosiery Museum** which forms part of the **Vauluisant Museum**, also housing the **Museum of Troyes & Champagne History**, in a former private mansion that was once the guest house of a Cistercian monastery. Rue Dominique. Open Wednesday to Sunday 10am to 12 noon and 2 to 6pm. (Tel: 03 25 73 05 85)

A Corner of Troyes
© CDT Aube

Shopping

Machine knitting, introduced to the city in the middle of the 18th century, is still its economic mainstay with some 200 companies directly employing around 10,000 people. Among the brands produced in the factories around Troyes are such leading names as Absorba, Adidas, Barbara, DD, Lacoste, Olympia and Petit Bateau. In the 1960s some of these manufacturers opened factory shops, initially to serve their own employees. The idea of buying leading brands at discounted prices attracted the rest of the population and soon people were coming in from far and wide.

© McArthur Glen / CDT Aube

Eventually these factory outlets became major shopping attractions and today there are no less than ten with the largest being found to the north east, in the Pont-Ste-Marie area, and to the south at St-Julien-les-Villas. They have now become giant shopping malls offering top brands like Armani, Versace, Cacharel, Timberland, Pol, Ralph Lauren, Nike and Mexx at up to 70% less than they were in the shops the previous season. The best time to go is in June or January when these factory outlets have special promotions; a good enough reason for British shopaholics to enjoy a few days R & R in Troyes! So popular has this style of shopping become that some of the centres run regular Saturday coach trips from Paris.

Food & Drink

Troyes is home to one of the strangest of all gourmet dishes, a tripe sausage made from chitterlings, or pigs intestines, the *Andouillette*. The very best are categorised A.A.A.A.A. which stands for *l'Association Amicale des Amateurs d'Andouillette de l'Aube* (The Friendly Association of lovers of Authentic Andouillette of the Aube); but be warned, they are very much an acquired taste!

Christopher Thierry is one of the leading craftsman-producers of this strange delicacy and, although his English is limited, he welcomes visitors by appointment to his shop. He takes them into what he calls his laboratory where he and his small, dedicated team produce top quality Andouillette. He only uses intestines from organically-bred pigs from Brittany and following extensive washing they are cut and dressed by hand, not minced like lesser commercially available versions. They are then cooked with seasoned onions, mustard and white wine, salt and pepper before they are strung out, cut to length and then fed by hand like so many shoe laces through pig gut sheathes. His *Andouillette* are sold all over France from Paris to Marseilles and you'll find them by name on the menus of the top restaurants throughout the Aube. 27, Ave. Galliéni, Sainte-Savine, to the west of the city. (Tel: 03 25 79 08 74)

The Museum of Tools & Working Class Thought, Troyes
© D. Le Neve/CDT Aube

True enthusiasts enjoy their Andouillette with a sauce made from fresh cream, white wine, French mustard and shallots. At home M. Thierry cooks his in a pan with a little butter, pork and wild mushrooms that he accompanies with a bottle of his favourite Rosé de Riceys. They can also be served as brochette with a mustard sauce, baked on a barbecue in aluminium foil or even cooked and cut into slices and served as appetisers to accompany apéritifs.

Eating out in Troyes is always a pleasure with the Michelin-starred **Bourgogne** showing the way through menus that follow in the grand tradition of French *haut-cuisine*. Close to the market hall at 40, rue Gen. De Gaulle. Closed 27th July to 26th Aug., Sunday

© CDT Champagne Ardenne

(except from 15th Oct. to 20th June) and Monday. (Tel: 03 25 73 02 67)

In spite of being built in what was once a cinema, **Bistroquet** is a stylish restaurant that manages to recall a Paris brasserie of *La belle Epoque*. Eat outside in summer. Pl. Langevin. Closed Sunday, except at lunchtime from Sept. to June. (Tel: 03 25 73 65 65)

Among the best addresses in the city is **Le Valentino**, a smart restaurant adjacent to the hotel Relais St-Jean. In summer you can eat in the courtyard. 35, rue Paillot de Montabert. (Tel: 03 25 73 36 13)

Le Valentino
© *Moleda/CDT Aube*

Almost next door you'll find **Le Jardin Gourmand** which specialises in Andouillette de Troyes. The locals enjoy theirs simply cooked in a *chaource* (cheese) sauce and washed down with a glass or two of the delicious regional cider. 31, rue Paillot de Montabert. (Tel: 03 25 73 36 13)

Aux Crieures de Vin (a *crieur* is a newspaper seller) is a friendly wine bar where each noon and evening the menu of the day selected fresh from the market is chalked up on a board. Place Jean Jaurès. (Tel: 03 25 40 01 01)

Hotels

The leading city-centre hotels are in the de-luxe category. The exquisite **Champ des Oiseaux** (field of birds) beside the cathedral is a sympathetically restored 15th and 16th century half-timbered building. It was opened in 1995 by Mme. Monique Boisseau, a retired French teacher. No restaurant or car parking but a magically tranquil place to stay with most attentive staff. No lifts. 20, rue Linard-Gonthier. (Tel: 03 25 80 58 50 E-mail: message@champsdeoiseaux.com)

Le Champs des Oiseaux
© *Fr Guenet/CDT Aube*

Next door is the equally excellent **Maison de Rhodes**, opened in 2003 by Mme. Boisseua's son Thierry Carcassin, which is perhaps a shade more masculine and minimalist than its sister establishment. Some of the bathrooms can only be described as

© CDT Champagne Aube

palatial while in part the décor reflects its 18th century wood panelling with the red stain used on the beams in those days. Limited restaurant, served in the garden in summer, sensational breakfast. Small secure car park. No lifts. 18, rue Linard-Gonthier. (Tel: 03 25 43 11 11
E-mail: message@maisonderhodes.com)

Behind the half-timbered façade of the **Relais St-Jean** is a splendidly equipped, modern, well-run hotel with spacious rooms and large well-lit bathrooms. Direct access to an underground car park is a special bonus. This city centre hotel has no restaurant but is next door to Le Valentino. Excellent bar and even a bar-billiards table. 51, rue Paillot de Montabert. Closed 23rd Dec to 1st Jan. (Tel: 03 25 73 89 90
E-mail: infos@relais-st-jean.com)

Hotel de la Poste is a popular city centre hotel with well-fitted rooms and a separate excellent restaurant, *Les Gourmets*, which only closes Saturday midday. Service in both the hotel and restaurant is polished and professional.
35 rue Emile Zola. (Tel: 03 25 73 05 05
E-mail: reservations@hotel-de-la-poste.com)
Restaurant: 5 rue Poincaré. (Tel: 03 25 73 80 78)

M. & Mme. De Vos will welcome you to the **Royal Hôtel** on the leafy Boulevard Carnot. The pleasing rooms of this mid-range hotel are well insulated from the noise of the passing traffic while their elegant Louis Philippe-style restaurant offers a choice of classic and regional dishes. 22, Blvd. Carnot. (Tel: 03 25 73 19 99
E-mail: reservation@royal-hotel-troyes.com)

Fresh Air & Fun

Leave Troyes to the east on the N19 Chaumont road, cross over the autoroute and within 9km turn left at Lusigny-sur-Barse and you are in the **Parc Natural Regional de la Forêt d'Orient**, once owned by the Knights Templar. It is a truly splendid regional natural park of some 70,000ha with three man-made lakes covering 5,000ha. These lakes form reservoirs for the rivers Seine and Aube, stopping flooding in winter and providing much needed water in the dry summer months.

© CDT Champagne Ardenne

The largest is the *Lac Orient* whose 2,000ha are reserved for fishing and small sailing boats; night fishing for carp is a speciality. The marina for 250 craft at Mesnil-St-Pierre Port is a sailor's and wind-surfer's paradise, as well as providing sailing and diving schools; while around the lake are three sandy beaches that appeal to families with small children. The northerly part of *Lac Orient* and the southern part of the *Lac du Temple*, named after the Knights Templar, form a major bird sanctuary where some 265 species can be spotted by keen 'twitchers.' The *Lac Amance*, to the north, is where you'll find the powerboats, jet-skis and water-skiing prohibited on the other two lakes.

© CDT *Champagne Ardenne*

Families from all over Europe come to this nature park with their tents, caravans or trailer homes, complete with family boats, canoes and bicycles to holiday at well-appointed camping sites. Bicycles are a wonderful way of discovering the park and a special 42km *Voie Verte* (green route) cycle path has been laid out from Troyes to Port Dienville beside the canals leading to the forest. This is the safe and healthy way to travel and if you don't have a bike you can hire one.

© CDT *Champagne Ardenne*

Tiny hamlets and villages, some with beautiful half-timbered churches, are scattered around the forest to surprise cyclists and walkers and provide a welcome break. The church at Mathaux in the north of the park is particularly fine with perhaps the ones at Longsols and Lentilles, in the north, being the most spectacular.

To the north of the park is **Brienne le Château** which was once the home of one of France's oldest noble families. In 1776 it became one of the twelve military preparatory schools set up to serve the Royal Military School in Paris. Between 1779 and 1784 the young Napoleon Bonaparte was a student here and a museum recalls his stay. Napoleon returned on 29th January 1814 to fight two of his last battles on French soil-the first at Brienne and two days later at La Rothière.

You don't have to camp as there are numerous *chambres d'hôte*, inns and small hotels in the park. ***L'Auberge de la Plaine*** at **La**

Auberge de la Plaine
© CDT Champagne Aube

Rothière, south of Brienne le Château on the D396, is a simple, restful roadside inn whose bedrooms and restaurant are in keeping with its peasant tradition. Closed 19th to 29th Dec., Wednesday night and Saturday midday between 23rd Sept and end of June. (Tel: 03 25 92 21 79 E-mail: aubergedelaplaine@wanadoo.fr)

The *Vieux Logis* (the old dwelling) is a pleasing inn with five en-suite rooms at Brévonnes at the north west corner of the park. The family atmosphere is jealously preserved with rustic furniture and trinkets adding to the illusion that you are in your grandmother's home. The chef/patron, Daniel Baudesson, is a true disciple of Escoffier and on certain Saturdays throughout the year runs a series of day-long cookery classes. Closed 1st to 24th March, Monday except the night during the season and Sunday night. (Tel: 03 25 46 30 17)

Marie-Christine and Patrick Gublin own *L'Auberge du Lac au Vieux Pressoir* (The inn of the lake with the old wine press) at Mesnil-St-Père, to the south east of the park. This is an excellent restaurant with pretty, well-equipped bedrooms. Those in the main house are a little on the small side while the larger rooms in the annexe lack some of their charm. The spacious restaurant spreads

L'Auberge du Lac
© Moleda/CDT Aube

out into the garden in summer for *Al Fresco* dining. Patrick Gublin's classic menus are elegantly prepared and professionally served. Closed 12th to 30th Nov. Sunday night from Oct. to mid-March and Monday midday. (Tel: 03 25 41 57 59 E-mail: auberge.lac.p.gublin@wanadoo.fr)

Bar-sur-Aube

Some 25km from Mesnil-sur-Père, on the main road to
Chaumont, you will see signs to **Nigloland** – the
kingdom of the small hedgehog. This 18ha theme
park, hidden away in the valley of the river Landion, is
one of the most visited attractions in France after
Disney and Asterix. It offers a range of 32 rides and
other activities that includes a terrifying ride on the Bat
Coaster when you can experience forces of up to 4G
upside down! Or relax on a Mississippi style stern-wheel
paddleboat listening to Trad Jazz while sipping a 'mint
julep' or glass of champagne. Nigoland even has its own
Pirate Hotel with 70 suitably themed bedrooms.
(Tel: 03 25 27 94 52 E-mail: contact@nigoland.fr)
Website: www.nigoland.fr

Nigloland
© Moleda/CDT Aube

Set in the vineyards close to to Nigloland is *The
Moulin du Landion*. This attractive hotel's
gourmet restaurant is over the water mill from
which it takes its name. Well proportioned
comfortable rooms, swimming pool and plenty of
car parking space. M & Mme. Heckmann. 5, rue
St-Léger, Dolancourt. (Tel: 03 25 27 92 17
E-mail: moulindulandion@wanadoo.fr)

The Moulin du Landion
© CDT Aube

Bar-sur-Aube is the principle town of the area.
For over 700 years **Bayel**, 8km to the south and
east on the D386,
has been a
centre of
glassmaking
excellence and supplied wares that
were much in demand at the great
champagne fairs of Troyes.
Craftsmen also sold their glass to
the royal household and became
known as Gentlemen-
Glassmakers, an early French
equivalent of the British Royal
Warrant.

In 1663 Queen Maria Theresa,
the Spanish wife of Louis XIV,
sent for some glassmakers from
Murano, in Italy, to produce

© CDT Champagne Ardenne

crystal for the royal household. In 1666, led by J.B Mazzolay, they were given permission to call their Paris factory the Manufacture Royale de Champagne. By 1679 they had become French citizens and settled in Bayel where there was a good supply of sand for silica, ferns for potash and wood to fire the furnace. In 1892, under the management of Henri Meissirel and Louis Marquot, the company changed its name to Cristalleries Royales de Champagne. By 1991 the wheel had turned full circle when the company was acquired by the Italian Borgosesia crystal glass group.

Today the factory still produces wide ranges of beautifully crafted stemware as well as elegant decanters and exquisite vases. There are daily tours of the glass works where you can see the whole process that turns molten glass into hand-blown products. There is also a museum of glass making and a factory shop where you can buy examples of the products that have been made on the site for over 325 years. Visits Monday to Saturday 9.15am to 1pm and 2 to 6.30pm. 1st April to 30th Sept. Also Sundays between 2 to 6pm from 1st April to 30th Sept. Office de Tourisme 2, rue Bell Verrière. (Tel: 03 25 92 42 68 E-mail: ot.bayel@wanadoo.fr)

© Drappier Collection

Follow the main road for a further 6km and you will reach **Clairvaux** whose monastery was founded in 1115 by a monk who came originally from Troyes but learnt his profession in Burgundy. He returned to his homeland with eleven companions, all dedicated to God and hard work, and some red wine vines. That monk was to become St-Bernard, founder of the Cistercian order, and the monastery one of the most influential centres of religion in the whole of France. Much of the building was destroyed by the revolution and little now remains except for some ruins that can be visited on Saturdays. There is also a state prison, built during the Napoleonic period, where it is said the real Jean Valjean, the inspiration for Victor Hugo's *Les Misérables*, was imprisoned. The *Hostellerie des Dames*, built around 1500, is open for visits every afternoon from May to October. The 18th century church **Ville-sur-la-Ferté**, 4km down the road, houses some relics from the abbey including St-Bernard's shroud. (Tel: 03 25 27 52 55 E-mail: abbaye-clairvaux@barsuraube.net)

People from all over the world are attracted to the sleepy Haute-Marne village of **Colombey-les-Deux-Eglises** surmounted by its giant cross of Lorraine. This symbol of the Free French throughout the 1939-45 war is a memorial to Colombey's most famous resident – General Charles de Gaulle. It is interesting that in the 1930s both Sir Winston Churchill and de Gaulle bought family homes in strategic locations. Churchill's Chartwell is between London and Dover while de Gaulle chose La Boisserie – on the site of a former brewery – between Paris and Metz, which was then the HQ of France's Eastern Army.

© CDT Champagne Ardenne

Parts of the ground floor of this simple country house can be visited every day except Tuesday. It provides an exceptional insight into the uncomplicated family life of one of the last century's most outstanding leaders. He is buried with his wife and daughter in a plain, unadorned grave beside the village church. His final command, that there must be no plaques on his tomb, has been scrupulously obeyed. To make sure he rests in peace a *gendarme* stands vigil in his sentry box just beyond the churchyard gate. The tourist office, in the village, has a well-written informative leaflet in English on de Gaulle at Colombey.

The office is opposite the excellent **Auberge de la Montagne**; an idyllic Michelin-starred restaurant with rooms where chef/patron M. Natali prepares his seductive dishes with consummate skill. The eight very pretty rooms are superbly equipped and overlook a peaceful garden.

The village of **Rizacourt-Buchey** is deep among the vines that grow on the steep hillsides. Leaving Colombey on the D2 you follow signs for Pratz then take the D104 through Argentolles, bypassing Buchey until you come to Rizacourt. You'll find Jean-Jacques Dubanton on your left as you enter the village. He sends the fruit from his 4ha to the co-op in Bar-sur-Seine who return bottles of newly-blended wine for ageing, riddling and disgorging. As well as the **Monique Dubanton** brand he has a second string to his bow; this is **Champagne Amielie-Clement** named after his two children. Many of his wines appear to be over-sweet and short, perhaps the problem of over-dosing before putting in the final cork. However, his **Amielie-Clement** *Brut Prestige* makes the visit well worth while. Marked autolysis is followed by sweet hazelnuts, the champagne has a firm mouth-feel created by a good *mousse* and perceived weight on the tongue with a long sustained finish. Rue de la Haute-Fontaine. Visits by appointment. (Tel: 03 25 01 50 80)

There must be something ironic about a village called **Colombey-le-Sec** (the dry) that is brimming over with champagne producers! To get there you drive through Rizaucourt, leaving to the north-west on the D203 to Saulcy, keep on through this village towards Colombey-la-Fosse on the D13 where you turn left into Colombey-le-Sec. **Charles Clément** will be on your left as you drive through the village. This is an Auboise co-operative that was formed in 1956 by Charles Clément and a few friends who between them had 18ha. Today there are 70 active members with some 170ha and it is still growing.

With a capacity for producing 12,000hl of wine each year it's not surprising that this co-op's mainstay is selling base wine in bulk to the big merchant houses in Reims and Epernay. However, the champagnes they make and sell under their own label amply repay all the obvious care and attention they receive. The entry level Brut spends three years on its cork while vintage and *Grande Réserve* lie on their sides for at least five years. Balance, power and length are the hallmarks of these fine champagnes, and Belgians – who are both astute and frequent cellar door buyers throughout Champagne – can often be found here filling up the boots of their cars for the short journey home. Rue St-Antoine. Visits Tuesday to Saturday 8am to 12 noon and 1.30 to 5.30pm. From 15th June to 1st Sept. Open on Sundays 1.30 to 5.30pm. (Tel: 03 25 92 50 71 E-mail: champagne-charles-clement@wanadoo.fr)

© *Champagne Bureau*

It is now only a short drive back to Bar-sur-Aube and the hotel **Le St-Nicolas** whose large airy rooms, outdoor swimming pool and friendly bar provide a quiet haven for a night or two. No car parking and no lift to the first floor rooms. No restaurant but there are two quite excellent ones in the town. 2, rue du Général du Gaulle. (Tel: 03 25 27 08 65)

La Toque Baralbine (a toque is a chef's tall white hat) on the main street is very good indeed. Young chef/patron Daniel Phelizot adds innovative modern touches to traditional French cuisine while his charming wife, Sylvie, ensures that service is calm and efficient.

A Corner in the La Toque Baralbine

© *La Torque Baralbine*

A good, well-chosen wine-list. 18, rue Nationale. Closed 5th to 26th Jan. Sunday night and Monday. (Tel: 03 25 27 20 34 E-mail: toquebaralbine@aol.com)

The spectacular *Cellier aux Moines* (monks wine cellar), set in a magnificent 12th century arched cellar built by the monks of Clairvaux, specialises in serving lunches of regional dishes. Rustic furniture and serving staff, dressed in traditional vineyard workers costumes, add a sense of theatre to a visit. Rue Général Vouillemount. Closed Tuesday midday and every evening except Friday and Saturday. (Tel: 03 25 27 08 01)

Bernard Guillerand's Hostellerie *La Chaumière* (little thatched cottage) is at Arsonval, 6km out of Bar-sur-Aube towards Troyes on the N19. A rustic restaurant set among trees with extremely well-appointed rooms in what once were the stables. Excellent bar and restful gardens. Secure car parking. Bernard is a splendid host and speaks very good English. Closed 10th Dec to 20th Jan, Sunday night and Monday. (Tel: 03 25 27 91 02 E-mail: lachaumiere@pem.net)

Hostellerie La Chaumière
© *Moleda/CDT Aube*

If you are only going to visit one champagne producer in the Bar-sur-Aube region then it must be **Drappier** at **Urville**. They are proud to have supplied the de Gaulle family with its champagnes from the time that the young colonel and his wife first settled at Colombey-les-Deux-Eglises. To get to Urville leave Bar-sur-Aube on the road to Bayel but turn left on to the D70 through Baroville – it's around 25km.

The Drappier family comes from Reims but in 1808 Louis Drappier settled in Urville and began to plant vineyards that today extend over 50ha. In the early 1830s Georges Collot, the maternal grandfather of Michel Drappier who now heads this family enterprise, decided to

© *Drappier Collection*

plant Pinot Noir grapes from nearby Burgundy. The locals laughed at him and called him Papa Pinot, but today these black gapes make up 70% of Drappier vineyards and are an essential part of the overall champagne blend.

Like all good winemakers Michel Drappier knows that truly great wines are made in the vineyards. As a result they are all very carefully tended, following the *Lutte Raisonée* approach of no artificial fertilisers and only treating those vines that need it and then never with toxic chemicals. Equal care in the winery with ultra-slow, cool pressing, slow cool second fermentation and special barrel aged *liqueurs d'expédition* – which are added to the wine before the final cork is driven in – all ensure the creation of beautifully balanced, homogenous champagnes.

The Drappier family
© *Drappier Collection*

Drappier's cellars, the oldest in the Aube, were originally dug by Cistercian monks from the neighbouring abbey of Clairvaux. They provide the ideal environment for the bottles to rest on their sides for a minimum of four years so that the wine can feed off its lees.

Most leading champagne producers offer giant-sized bottles but anything over Jeroboam in size (four bottles) is invariably decanted and even then they only go up to Nebuchadnezzer (20 bottles). Because of the family's subtle way of making their wines, with the absolute minimum of sulphur, once opened they are prone to oxidise quickly. As a result Drappier do not decant at all but make their champagnes in all the usual big bottles and even go two better; they offer Primat (36 bottles) and Melchizedek (40 bottles).

Harvesting in 1898
© *Drappier Collection*

With such a source of excellent champagne on their doorstep it's not surprising that the de Gaulle family's cellars were always stocked with Drappier's Extra Dry Cuvée. On 18th June 1990, the 50th anniversary of de Gaulle's historic 'call to arms,' Drappier launched their own *Cuvée Charles de Gaulle* as homage to the great man. Made from a blend of 80% Pinot Noir and 20% Chardonnay, like the General it has a massive structure and powerful nose dominated by Pinot and – like his memory – an enduring length.

The most sought-after of all the Drappier champagnes is their beautifully balanced *Grande Sendrée*, which takes its name from a parcel of land that was covered with cinders (*cendrée*) after a fire which ravaged Urville in 1838. A spelling error slipped into the land registry, which is why today it's spelt with an 's' and not a 'c'. The oldest vines from this plot are harvested with great care and the wine, made only from the heart of the best pressed juice, is a blend of 55% Pinot Noir and 45% Chardonnay.

The quality of any champagne house is set not by its prestige wines, as important as they might be, but by its entry-level Brut. At Drappier this is *Carte d'Or*, made from a blend of 80 to 90% Pinot Noir, 5% Pinot Meunier and five to 15% Chardonnay which has spent four years in the cellar. Aromas of sweet briar and peach are followed in the mouth by flavours of peach, apricot and red fruits with the typical Drappier elegant, long finish. Rue des Vignes. Visits Monday to Friday 8am to 12 noon and 2 to 6pm. (Tel: 03 25 27 40 15 E-mail: info@champagne-drappier.com)

© *Champagne Drappier*

Leave Urville towards the west on the D44, turn left at the T junction beside the river Landion and within 4km you are in **Bligny** with its majestic château, one of only two in the whole of Champagne that actually makes champagne. Set in a magnificent 400ha park which includes 15ha of Pinot Noir and

Château de Bligny
© *CDT Aube*

Chardonnay vines, the château and its magnificent rooms appear to be more important than the champagne they produce! And this is a pity because, under the new owners, the quality of the wines has certainly improved.

However this handsome historic château, built in extravagant 19th century style, is well worth visiting to see the elegantly furnished reception rooms as well as ten quite spectacular bedrooms that come complete with 21st century bathrooms. There is also a fascinating collection of well over 100 old champagne glasses. Part of the old cellar has been turned into a vast function suite and the winery is now down in the old stables. Subject to availability you might be able to stay at the *Château de Bligny* but if you want to dine there they have to bring in a caterer, so the whole experience can be rather expensive. Open Monday to Saturday 10.30am to 6.30pm, subject to not being booked for a function. (Tel: 03 25 27 40 11)

Bar-sur-Seine

Leave Bligny on the D4 through Vitry and Equilly where you turn left on to the D79 towards **Essoyes**, a distance of some 18km. This pretty little town on the river Ource is where artist Pierre-Auguste Renoir (1841-1919) made his home and built a studio. A prodigious painter whose most famous works included *Le Bal du Moulin de la Galette* and *Le Déjeuner des Canotiers'*, he was first brought to Essoyes by Aline Charigot, his model and later his wife, who was born there. Renoir enjoyed living among winegrowers and found the countryside provided inspiration for his paintings. Visits most afternoons between 2 to 6.30pm from 15th May and 1st Nov. 7, rue Extra (Tel: 03 25 38 56 28)

A new museum is being built that will tell the twin stories of the vineyards and the Renoir family. A new hotel, the aptly named Hotel des Canotiers, welcomes visitors while there are several *chambres d'hôte* in the village.

© *Praliaud/CDT Aube*

The countryside between the rivers Arce and Ource is especially beautiful with verdant vineyards on the slopes of tree-topped, rolling hills with, in between, unspoilt villages like **Landreville** whose narrow lanes wind up to the vines and down to the river. Tucked away in the quietest back street you will find **La Val Fleurie** (valley of the flowers), Brigitte and Michel Henriot's blissfully comfortable *chambres d'hôte* set in a beautiful garden. Michel and his son are wine farmers and members of a local co-operative which sends wines up to Nicolas Feuillatte. If you arrange to have supper with them you'll probably eat in the garden and have one of the family's champagnes.

Brigitte is a Parisenne and speaks good English. 8, rue de la Vieille Halle. (Tel: 03 25 38 57 23)

At the other end of the village, close by the church, are **Robert Dufour & Fils** whose ancestors have been growing grapes since 1610. They have moved the winery away from the family home and converted the space it once occupied into a charming set of rooms to let together with a little boutique selling their wines and local produce. Robert and his son

Renoir's studio
© *Moleda/CDT Aube*

Charles, who speaks very good English, have 14ha of Pinot Noir and Chardonnay from which they make champagne as well as red and white *coteaux champenois* still wines. Their *cuvée selection*, made from equal parts of Chardonnay and Pinot Noir, bottled in 1995 and disgorged eight years later in 2003, is deliciously fresh, packed with brioche and ripe fruit. 4, rue de la Croix Malot. (Tel: 03 25 29 66 19 E-mail: champagnedufour@aol.com)

Vineyards
© *Champagne Robert Dufour*

Pierre-Eric Jolly of **Champagne René Jolly** is a winegrower with 10ha and masses of ambition. His *Brut Rosé* is suffused with red and black currants, while his nv *Blanc de Blancs* is full of aromas of butter and passion-fruit. Visits by appointment. 10, rue de la Gare. (Tel: 03 25 38 50 91)

As you drive across the hills between the villages look out for the little conical stone huts. These are *les Cadoles*, shelters built by the vineyard workers from stones found in the fields. Abandoned after the phylloxera outbreak at the end of the 19th century, today they are mostly found in old vineyards that have never been replanted.

Chambre d'hôte at Champagne Robert Dufour et Fils
© *Champagne Robert Dufour*

Ville sur Arce is one of these wine villages, set on the plain, which is full of champagne producers. **Rémy Massin & Fils** have been farming grapes since 1865 but only started to make champagnes in 1974. The well-made wines from their 20ha of vineyards have subtle structures showing an abundance of ripe fruit on the palate. Their *Cuvée Tradition, a blanc de noirs* made from a blend of Pinot Noir grapes harvested over three vintages, has an almost shy entry but develops with style and length. The family also has *chambres d'hôte* and makes something of a speciality of receiving guests during the harvest. 34, Grande Rue. Visits Monday to Friday office hours and Saturday mornings. (Tel: 03 25 38 74 09 E-mail: contact@champagne-massin.com)

The village also has its own co-operative, Champagne **Chassenay d'Arce** with some 130 growers. Here you will find out the history and methods of cultivating grapes as well as tasting champagnes sold in top UK supermarkets. (Tel: 03 25 38 30 70)

A corner of Bar sur Seine
© Ph Praliaud/CDT Aube

© CDT Aube

New wine-growing enterprises are the exception, not the rule, and the Brulez family from Noé-les-Mallets is exceptional in more ways than one. The two brothers and sister have named their champagnes after their maternal grandmother **Louise Brison**. They farm their 12ha of vineyard along strict *Lutte Raisonée* lines, using absolutely no artificial fertilisers or toxic herbicides, preferring short pruning, cattle manure and pheromones to confuse and de-sex flying parasites. Oenologist Francis Brulez believes in allowing his wines to express their *terroir* and fruit. He keeps his newly pressed juice for at least 18 hours in chilled tanks for the solids to precipitate before fermenting in thermo-regulated stainless steel tanks. He tries to make his base wine with sufficient acidity so that they will not require a malolactic conversion. His wines are then aged for up to six months in 250 litre oak barrels before blending and bottling. Entry level Brut will remain in the cellars for at least three years with the prestige *cuvées* for six years or more. The medieval roundel on their label recalls Ann Musinier, a beauty of her day who was born in Noé and became the mistress of Henri I, Count of Champagne (1152-1180). She saved his life during an attempted assassination and in return he gave her a title.

Louise Brison is a family of patrician champagnes that combine expressive biscuity aromas with a roundness and depth of fruit. Hameau du Grand Mallets, Noë les Mallets. Visits by appointment Monday to Friday during office hours. (Tel: 03 25 29 66 62 E-mail: champagne@louise-brison.fr)

The old walled town of **Bar-sur-Seine** is 33km out of Troyes on the N71. The *Hotel du Commerce* in the town square has a decent restaurant that in summer spreads across to tables on the adjacent town square. Modest rooms have more or less been refurbished. Rue République. Closed 25th to 31st Aug. Closed Sunday, except midday in July & Aug. and Wednesday. (Tel: 03 25 29 86 36)

If you continue down the main road for 4km you will see a giant cork on your left that announces the village of **Celles-sur-Ource**. This village's claim to fame is that it has 48 winegrowers producing some $1^1/_2$ million bottles a year, more than any other village in the whole of Champagne. Turn left and, as they say, you takes your pick and makes your choice. But do look for signs that they speak English,

There are a number of Cheurlins in the village and **Arnaud de Cheurlin** is owned and run by M. and Mme. Eisenträger; he is German and she was a Mlle. Cheurlin. They make some 50,000 bottles a year from their 6ha of vineyard. Their entry champagne is a *Blanc de Noir* made from equal parts of the two Pinots. Their rosé, made from Pinot Noir as a pink wine, is powerful and fruity. 58, Grande-Rue, Visits strictly by appointment, not a lot of English. (Tel: 03 25 38 53 90
E-mail: info@arnaud-de-cheurlin-champagne.com)

Richard Cheurlin is the fifth direct descendant of his family to grow grapes in the village. He makes clean and balanced wines from his 8.3ha that have a roundness from ageing the base wine in wooden barrels. 16, rue des Huguenots. Open Monday to Saturday. Visits by appointment. (Tel: 03 25 38 58 33
E-mail: richard.cheurlin@wanadoo.fr)

Champagne Marcel Vézien is a family business that has been run by the family for four generations. Tours in English with Marie José Vézien, The Grand Master of the Brotherhood of Saulte Bouchon, are great fun. He will show you their vaulted cellars and you will see the traditional wine presses that they still use today. At harvest time they also offer their visitors the opportunity to join them picking in the vineyards! (Tel: 03 25 38 50 22)

© *Champagne Bureau*

If you're seeking tales of the unexpected, then **Michel Furdyna** has them by the score. He knows more about this extraordinary village than anyone else and is delighted to share it all with you over a glass of his champagne. 13, rue Trot. Open every day except Sunday, but visits only by appointment. (Tel: 03 25 38 54 20
E-mail: champagne.furdyna@wanadoo.fr)

Rejoin the main road south that follows the Seine and in about 12km turn left towards **Courton**. On your left as you drive through the village is **Fleury Pere et Fils**, the first champagne

Vineyards in Winter
© *Champagne Bureau*

producer to become accredited as an organic grower and who has led the way with bio-dynamic vineyards.

In the early 1990s Jean-Paul Fleury, a fourth generation champagne producer, decided to convert to biodynamic winemaking. This holistic approach embraces completely organic cultivation and goes further, stressing among other things planetary influences on the vineyard. Says Jean-Paul, "You can see the difference in the vineyard with your eyes and taste the difference in the *cuvées*. The vines devote more energy to the grapes and give more character and complexity to the wine".

Jean-Paul makes his wines from 13ha that he farms, half of which belongs to his family and the balance shared with colleagues. His wines are all aged in oak barrels and, after blending, the bottles are closed with real corks, not metal crown corks, while they rest on their sides. His non-vintage Brut is full of complex and potent flavours and numbers the highly influential American wine critic, Robert Parker, among its fans. *Tradition Carte Rouge* is a *blanc de noirs* with powerful well-developed complex aromas of honey, acacia, wax and toast. 43, Grande Rue. Visits strictly by appointment. (Tel: 03 25 38 20 28
E-mail: champagne-fleury@wanadoo.fr.)

Continue driving through the village and at Gyé-sur-Seine turn left on to the D70; after crossing the main road continue the 8km to Les Riceys.

Les Riceys

Rosé de Riceys we're told,
Gets better as it gets old.
A pink delicate wine
That's serenely sublime
With Andouillette, pungent and bold.

The commune of Les Riceys is made up of three pretty villages, Ricey Haut, Haute-Rive and Ricey Bas. They lie at the southern tip of Champagne and are far closer climatically and geographically to Burgundy than to Reims. It is the only commune in the whole of the champagne region allowed to make three appellations; champagne, *Coteaux Champenois* and *Rosé des Riceys*, Louis XIV's favourite wine. Although there are 350 growers in Ricey, only 40 of them make Rosé des Riceys.

This extraordinary wine with its bouquet of wild flowers, violets and hazelnuts can only be made in dry harvests from Pinot Noir from specially designated vineyards that must achieve a potential alcohol level of 10° before picking. The best bunches are laid on the floor of an open vat. The bottom level was traditionally trodden by foot and then the vat filled up with whole unbroken bunches. The yeast on the skin of the grapes would start to ferment the juice and the process which turns grape juice into wine had begun.

Ricey Bas
© *M. Besnier/CDT Aube*

After the fermentation has started whole bunches are placed in the vat and the fermenting juice is pumped over them. During this critical period the winemakers live with their vats so that they can be there at the precise moment when the aromas and flavours are judged to be correct. Only then is the free-run juice run off and the grapes pressed. The young wine is then blended and held for at least a year in old oak barrels. It is bottled as a still rosé with all the colour of a tropical sunset.

Young Rosé des Riceys is a delightful apéritif but as it ages it develops powerful Burgundian flavours that enable it to accompany *charcoute* as well as A.A.A.A.A Andouillette.

Christophe Defrance
© Ph. Praliaud

Christophe Defrance, of **Jacques Defrance**, is seldom in the family's vaulted 13th century cellars. He is usually found high in the hills among the vines from which he creates impeccable champagnes and outstanding Rosé des Riceys. Christophe is the fourth generation of his family to make both champagne and Rosé des Riceys from its 10ha of vines. Eight of these are Pinot Noir but only 2½ha of them are in the small area designated for producing Rosé de Riceys.

Defrance champagnes are exceptionally well made with rich fruity flavours that come from a prevalence of Pinot Noir. However, it is the rare Rosé des Riceys that is the most sought-after of all the family's wines. It is not surprising that the family regularly exports a good third of its annual production. 28, rue de la Plante, Ricey Bas. € Visits only by appointment, very little English. (Tel: 03 25 29 32 20)

Gallimard Père & Fils has been selling its own champagne since 1930. Before that the family sold their still wines made from their grapes to producers in the Marne. Didier Gallimard is the fifth generation of his family to be in the business which today comprises some 10ha of their own vineyards – they buy-in additional grapes and juice from other growers – with five million bottles lying in their cellars. The non-vintage champagnes rest for a minimum of 24 months while the vintage stay at least twice as long.

All the champagnes are given a malolactic conversion and are deliciously refreshing, fine and floral with some considerable finesse. In time they develop attractive biscuity aromas and flavours. The beautifully balanced *blanc de noirs* non-vintage *Cuvée Réserve* has ample flavours of freshly plucked red currants. A five-year-old *Cuvée Réserve* made from 65% Pinot Noir and 35% Chardonnay was wonderfully round with a combination of honey and quince.

© Champagne Bureau

The Rosé des Riceys is made in open tanks from vines that are at least 40 years old. The grapes are allowed to ferment for between two and five days. Contrary to tradition their wine then spends a year in a stainless steel tank which protects its light and fresh flavours which the family feel would be dumbed-down by barrel ageing. After five years in the bottle the wine will have developed aromas of strawberry conserve with flavours of wild strawberries and quince. 18-20, rue Gaston Cheq, Le Magny. € Visits Monday to Friday 9am to 12 noon and 2 to 5.30pm. (Tel: 03 25 29 32 44)

Dominating the scene in Les Riceys is the merchant house of **Alexandre Bonnet** who unfortunately do not receive casual visitors. Founded in 1932 by the Bonnet family, today it is a member of the BCC group and a major source of excellent Pinot Noir-based Blanc de Noirs. In addition they send a great deal of pressed juice and base Pinot Noir wine up to Reims and Epernay and, in return, take Chardonnay from the Marne for blending in with their own champagnes.

Hotel Magny provides that winning combination of comfortable, rustic accommodation with a welcoming heated outdoor swimming pool and a restaurant serving well-prepared traditional dishes and excellent inexpensive champagne. Plenty of car parking. No lift to first floor rooms. Friendly small bar. On the D252. Closed Jan., Feb. and 25th to 28th Aug., Sunday night, Tuesday night Oct. to April and Wednesday, except at night from May to Sept. (Tel: 03 25 29 38 39)

Hotel Magny
© Huyghens Danrigal/C.I.V.C Collection

You could return directly to Troyes but why not drive the 28km across country on the D17 towards Chaource, the town from which champagne's leading cheese takes its name. Turn left at Pargues (22km from Les Riceys) for **Maisions-les-Chaource** and stay at **Aux Maisons**, a big former champagne farm which has been turned into a comfortable country hotel with a swimming pool, well sound-insulated rooms and a restaurant serving interesting, simple dishes. An ideal place to end your champagne odyssey.

Aux Maisons
© D. Le Neve/CDT Aube

Tasting Champagne

You really can never go wrong
With the blanc de blancs from Salon.
You're life won't be wasted
If once you have tasted
Those flavours that go on and on.

There is only one way to assess the quality of champagne-
and that is to drink it. The bottle should be lightly chilled;
20 minutes in an ice bucket with one-third ice and two-
thirds cold tap water does the job perfectly or add some salt if you
want to speed it up. If it is too cold you will mask the wine's
subtle flavours.

Open the bottle with care by holding it in a napkin to get a good
grip and first remove the wire muzzle, keeping a thumb securely
over the cork all the time. Hold the bottle at a slight angle and
firmly twist the bottle – never the cork. The cork should free
itself, gently rising under the pressure of the gas inside. Rock
the cork gently and carefully to allow the excess gas to escape
discreetly.

A bottle of champagne should be opened with no more sound
than that of a maiden's sigh. Loud 'pops' or the vulgar displays

© *Champagne Bureau*

seen after Grand Prix races are quite definitely out. If you have a cork that just refuses to move then either use special champagne pincers to grip the cork while you turn the bottle or place the neck under running hot water; but hang on to the cork as it could fly out!

Pour a little wine, sufficient to fill a quarter of the glass, into a dry and clean crystal-clear flute or tulip. When the bubbles subside, fill the glass up to no more than two-thirds. Any dampness or vestiges of washing up liquid will kill the bubbles, as indeed do certain high-gloss lipsticks. Look at the cork, the straighter the cork, the longer since the wine was disgorged while wide spreading 'skirts' indicate more recent disgorging.

© Champagne Bureau

Examine the *mousse*, the white frothy head – does it hold up well? Study the bubbles. They should form a constant and consistent flow of minuscule spheres floating serenely to the surface.

Now put your nose into the top of the glass to savour the aromas before sipping the wine and discovering all its enigmatic charms. You should try and get the wine to all the 9,000 taste buds that lie along your tongue. Those at the front detect sugar and glucose sweetness; they are followed by those that respond to salt, fructose and bitter flavours; with those that react to sourness and acidity at the back. Marked acidity is often the sign of a young wine that requires more ageing.

© Champagne Bureau

Oh, and if you would like to, spit – but with champagne it's not mandatory!

Flute or Saucer – which is the best style of glass for enjoying champagne?

'A glass or two does you no harm',
Said the man from the House of Grande Dame.
And this he should know,
For the widow Clicquot
Made champagne that oozes with charm.

© Drappier Collection

Champagne wasn't always crystal-clear. Before *la Veuve Clicquot* cut her kitchen table in half and had holes drilled in it to make the first *pupître*, champagnes had bubbles but they were invariably cloudy with sediment. To help clean them up they were drunk out of deep beakers that looked more like small lager glasses with a globe at the base into which the sediment would eventually fall. Indeed, in those early days champagne was invariably decanted.

Today this is only done for old vintage sweet champagnes that can produce harmless clear crystals of tartaric acid. However, Michel Drappier has recently designed a special decanter for vintage wines that may be closed and need aerating to open them up. He is having them made at the one-time royal glassworks at Bayel, only 15km from the Drappier cellars in Urville.

After the Widow's innovation, champagne was at last crystal-clear. The *beau monde* of Paris were so eager to show that they were drinking the new-style champagne that they had special glasses made. These were the infamous saucers which remained popular in Britain and the US until the early 1960s. Legend tells us that these were modelled on the bosoms of Madame de Pompadour, the mistress of Louis XV and for a long time the real ruler of France.

During the *art-déco* period opaque and decorated saucers became all the rage. These made it absolutely impossible to see the bubbles, let alone the colour of the wine. Another fashionable horror of the

© Drappier Collection

age was the silver or gold swizzle stick that was used to remove the bubbles!

And then common sense won through and the flute or tulip glass became the accepted drinking vessel for champagne.

The perfect champagne glass should have a long stem with a tall tulip-shaped tapering bowl. Ideally it should be made from the thinnest of lead crystal with absolutely no colour or decoration. This allows the wine to show itself off to maximum advantage so that you can enjoy the luxuriant *mousse*, subtle colour and enchanting display of tiny pinprick-sized bubbles. It should never be filled more than half to two-thirds. This allows the top of the tapering bowl to capture all the wine's delicate aromas and hold them there for you to savour. It is a strange fact but the majority of champagne glasses actually have a fault in the bottom of the bowl that encourages the bubbles to rise from the bottom.

You should always hold your champagne glass, or indeed any wineglass, by the base and never by the bowl. This is because the warmth of your hand is more than sufficient to raise the temperature of the wine.

Michael Drappier uses his new decanter for vintage champagne
© *Philippe Boucheron*

Leading champagne producing groups

Louis Vuiton Moët Hennessy	Moët & Chandon, Veuve Clicquot Ponsardin, Ruinart, Krug, Mercier
Marne-et-Champagne	Lanson, Besserat de Bellefon, Massé, Gauthier, Alfred Rothschild
Vranken-Pommery-Monopole	Pommery, Demoiselle, Barancourt, Charles Lafitte, Charbaut, Heidsieck Monopol, Vranken
Laurent-Perrier	Laurent-Perrier, Delamotte, Salon, De Castellane
Allied Domecq	Mumm, Perrier-Jouët
Rémy-Cointreau	Piper Heidsieck, Charles Heidsieck
Roederer	Roederer, Deutz, Théophile Roederer
BCC	Boizel, Bonet, Chanoine, Philipponnat
Taittinger	Tattinger, Irroy

Glossary of champagne terms

Balthazar	Large 12 litre bottle containing 16 x 75 cl bottles
Blanc de Blancs	White wine made exclusively from white grapes
Blanc de Noirs	White wine made exclusively from black grapes
Brut	Dry champagne with less than 15 g/l of residual sugar
Brut Nature	Very dry champagne with less than 3 g/l of residual sugar
Chef-de-Caves	Cellar master and winemaker
Clos	Enclosed vineyards
Cru	Growth, often indicates a named vineyard
Cuvée	First 2,050 litres of juice from a 4,000kg **Marc** or finished blend made up from numerous **Crus**
Dégorgement	Removal of dead yeast sediment from the bottle
Demi-Sec	Sweet champagne with 33 to 50 g/l of residual sugar
Dosage	Sugar cane syrup in the **Liqueur d'expédition**
Doux	Very sweet champagne with more than 50 g/l of residual sugar
Dry or Sec	Medium-sweet wine with 17 to 35 g/l of residual sugar
Extra Brut	Dry champagne with between 0 and 6 g/l of residual sugar
Extra Dry or Sec	Medium-dry wine with 12 to 20 g/l of residual sugar
Grand Cru	Champagne from a 100% Grande Cru village
Grande Marque	Describes a large merchant house, or big brand
Gyropallet	Riddling machine, often computer controlled
Jeroboam	A double **Magnum** – 3 litres or 4 x 75 cl bottles
Liqueur d'expédition	Solution of cane sugar and wine to top up after **dégorgement**
Liqueur de tirage	Solution of yeast and sugar to provoke second fermentation in the bottle
Magnum	A double bottle containing 150 cl, the ideal size for any wine
Marc	4,000 Kg load of grapes for pressing
Methusalem	Six litre bottle holding 8 x 75 cl bottles
Milésime	Vintage
Nebuchadnezzar	15 litre giant containing 20 x 75 cl bottles
Non Vintage (NV)	Wines made from blend using **reserve wine**
Prise de mousse	Second fermentation in the bottle
Pupître	Hinged board for holding up to 60 bottles for the **remuage**
Remuage	Hand riddling bottles to collect sediment in the neck
Reserve wine	Still wines held over from previous years for blending
Salmanazar	Nine litre bottle or 12 x 75 cl bottles
Terroir	The combined effect of the soils, aspect to sun and microclimate within a vineyard
Vintage	Champagne made from wines harvested in a single year

Useful Addresses

Tourist Boards

London   French Tourist Office   178, Piccadilly W1J 9AL
Tel: 020 7399 3535
Website: www.franceguide.com

France   Aube   34, Quai Damperierre Troyes 10000
Tel: 03 25 42 50 00
Website: www.aube-champagne.com

Epernay   7, Ave. de Champagne 5120
Tel: 03 26 53 35 86
E-mail: tourisme@ot-epernay.fr

Hautvillers   Place de la République, 51160
Tel: 03 26 57 06 35
E-mail: contact@hautvillers.fr

Marne   13 bis, rue Carnot Charlons-en-Champagne 51006
Tel: 03 26 68 37 52
Website: www.tourisme-en-champagne.com

Reims   12, Blvd. Du Gen. Leclerc 51100
Tel: 03 2677 45 00
E-mail: tourismreims@netvia.com

Sézanne   Place de la République BP21 51120
Tel: 03 26 80 51 43
E-mail: tourisme.sezanne@wanadoo.fr

These tourist offices will also be able to tell you about special low and mid-season offers that provide discounted travel and hotel packages. They will also send you up-to-date brochures in English.

Fancy the idea of a champagne tour, but would rather have someone else arrange it all for you? Then talk to Arblaster & Clarke Wine Tours, Clarke House, Farnham Rd, West Liss, Hants. GU33 6JQ. (Tel: 01 730 893 344 E-mail: sales@winetours.co.uk
Website: www.winetours.co.uk)

Bibliography
Or – Don't leave home without them

Bibliography is a pretentious word that simply means other books on the subject. These have been divided into two – books you Must Have On Voyage, and for those seeking to learn more about *le champagne*, Should Have on Voyage.

Must Have on Voyage

Good French dictionary

Michelin Le guide rouge Red Guide to hotels and restaurants, always have the current edition.

Michelin Maps of the regions to be visited, or current **Tourist & Motoring Atlas of France.**

Gault Millau Guide An idiosyncratically written guide to restaurants and hotels, but you will need to have pretty good French to appreciate it. Again make sure that it is the current edition.

Should Have on Voyage

Hachette French Wine Guide English edition, an informative guide to some 9,000 of the best wines in France – the sommeliers (wine-waiters) 'bible'.

LexiWine/LexiVin A pocket book-sized English/French and French/English dictionary of over 5,000 technical and commercial wine words and phrases.

Tom Stevenson's Champagne Encyclopaedia of Champagne & Sparkling Wine.

Simply, the best book on the subject.

© *Drappier Collection*

Index

**Figures in italics refer to illustrations.
See also Glossary**

Philippe Boucheron

© Tom Bader

Wine is a way of life for Philippe Boucheron. Since the mid-1970s he has been writing on the subject and in 1987 he began broadcasting, organising tastings and even taking groups to vineyards as far apart as Champagne and the Cape.

He was the 1996 Wine Guild of the United Kingdom's Regional Wine Writer of the Year.

A former vice-chairman of The Circle of Wine Writers he is dedicated to improving the standards of communication about wines and spirits. He is also committed to promoting awareness of the health giving properties of red wine.

A keen advocate for maintaining the balance of nature, Philippe is an enthusiastic supporter of both organic and biodynamic wines.

A regular after-dinner speaker Philippe knows that people learn more by being entertained than by being talked at. As a result his talks, tastings and wine trips can be fascinating, sometimes even hilarious, but always informative.

I tell you, it's absolute folly
To get stinking on tonic and Stolly'
The truly well-bred
Retires to her bed,
With a bloke, and some bottles of Bolly'.